RK-021
MASSIMILIANO AFIERO

LEIBSTANDARTE PANZERS 1940-1945

Massimiliano Afiero

Leibstandarte Panzers 1940-1945

Leibstandarte Panzers 1940-1945 - By Massimilliano Afiero. RK021-EN First Edition June 2025 by Luca Cristini Editore per i tipi Soldiershop - Ritterkreuz Special.
Cover & Art Design by Soldiershop factory. ISBN code: 979125589-2519 Tank profile by Luca Cristini ©
First published by Luca Cristini Editore, copyright © 2025. No part of this publication may be reproduced, stored in a retrieval system or transmitted by any form or by any means, electronic, recording or otherwise without the prior permission in writing from the publishers. The publisher remains to disposition of the possible having right for all the doubtful sources images or not identifies. Visit www.soldiershop.com to read more about all our books and to buy them.

In merito alle serie Ritterkreuz e The Axis Forces ecc. l'editore Soldiershop informa che non essendone l'autore ne il primo editore del materiale pervenuto per la stesura del volume, declina ogni responsabilità in merito al suo contenuto di testi e/o immagini e la sua correttezza. A tal proposito segnaliamo che la pubblicazione Ritterkreuz tratta esclusivamente argomenti a carattere storico-militare e non intende esaltare alcun tipo di ideologia politica presente o del passato cosi come non intende esaltare alcun tipo di regime politico del secolo precedente ed alcuna forma di razzismo.

Leibstandarte Panzers 1940-1945

PzKpfw.IV '521' engaged in combat during Operation '*Zitadelle*' (NA).

Leibstandarte Panzers 1940-1945

The *Leibstandarte Adolf Hitler* was the first unit of the *Waffen-SS* and was also one of the first SS divisions to be equipped with armored vehicles as early as 1940, during its reorganization after the French campaign, when it was assigned a number of assault guns that had their baptism of fire during the Balkan campaign in the spring of 1941 to be later also engaged in the early stages of Operation Barbarossa on the Russian Southern Front. With the new reorganization of the unit into an armored grenadier division in the fall of 1942, the unit was provided with a full armored regiment equipped with *PzKpfw.III* and *PzKpfw.IV* and also a heavy armored company equipped with the new *PzKpfw.VI 'Tiger I'*. The division's new armored units then participated in the furious fighting to recapture Kharkov and Bjelgorod and the subsequent offensive against the Kursk salient. Transferred in the summer of 1943 to Italy because of the sudden Italian defection, Sepp Dietrich's division, after being engaged in disarming Royal Army troops and in some anti-partisan operations in Istria, returned to the Eastern Front to be engaged in new and hard offensive and defensive fighting. During this period, the armored regiment received the new *Panther* tanks. *The Panzers* and the men of the *Leibstandarte* contested every inch of ground against the Soviets with doggedness and determination, earning them numerous decorations for valor. After fighting on the Eastern Front in the Berditchev and Vinnitza area, the SS divisions in the spring of 1944 were transferred to Belgium for reorganization and especially to be engaged as a counterforce for the impending Allied landings on the continent. In June 1944, the division was then transferred to the Caen area where *Hitlerjugend* units were already fighting to counter the Allied offensive. In August 1944 The division's armored divisions participated in the counteroffensive on Mortain and then fell back eastward, fighting hard to get out of the Falaise pocket. After retreating into Germany, after a new and brief reorganization, the SS divisions participated in the offensive in the Ardennes, with *Kampfgruppe Peiper* at the tip of the spear. When the offensive ended, the division in January 1945 was transferred to the Hungarian front participating in the last German offensive actions of the war, and then fell back to Austria.

Massimiliano Afiero

The *PzKpfw.IV* '618' of the *Leibstandarte* at Piazza Duomo in Milan, summer 1943 (NARA).

I) The assault guns of the LSSAH

At the end of the French campaign in 1940, the units *of the Leibstandarte Adolf Hitler*[1] were transferred to the Metz area, as the unit, at that time with the status of a regiment, was to be transformed into a new motorized Brigade of the *Waffen-SS* by order of Hitler, who signed a decree on August 6 for its reinforcement. On August 19, 1940, the new Brigade was officially named as *Verstärkte*[2] *Leibstandarte SS Adolf Hitler*, with three new rifle battalions, a heavy weapons battalion, an artillery regiment and a scout battalion. In particular, the heavy weapons battalion was assigned six assault guns, *StuG III Ausf A*, which went to form a self-propelled gun battery, the *Panzer-Sturm-Batterie*, under the orders of *SS-Hstuf.* Georg Schönberger[3].

One of the first *StuG.IIIs* delivered to the *Leibstandarte* in 1940 (*Bundesarchiv*).

A *StuG.III* of the *Leibstandarte* in a Greek village.

In early 1941, the unit was renamed as *4.(StuG) Kompanie bei V.(schweren) Bataillon LSSAH*. Also commanding one of the assault guns was *SS-Uscha.* Michael Wittmann[4]. The *Leibstandarte* assault guns were first engaged during the Balkan campaign on the Greek front. Once operations were over, in May 1941 the units were transferred to Brno, in the Protectorate of Bohemia and

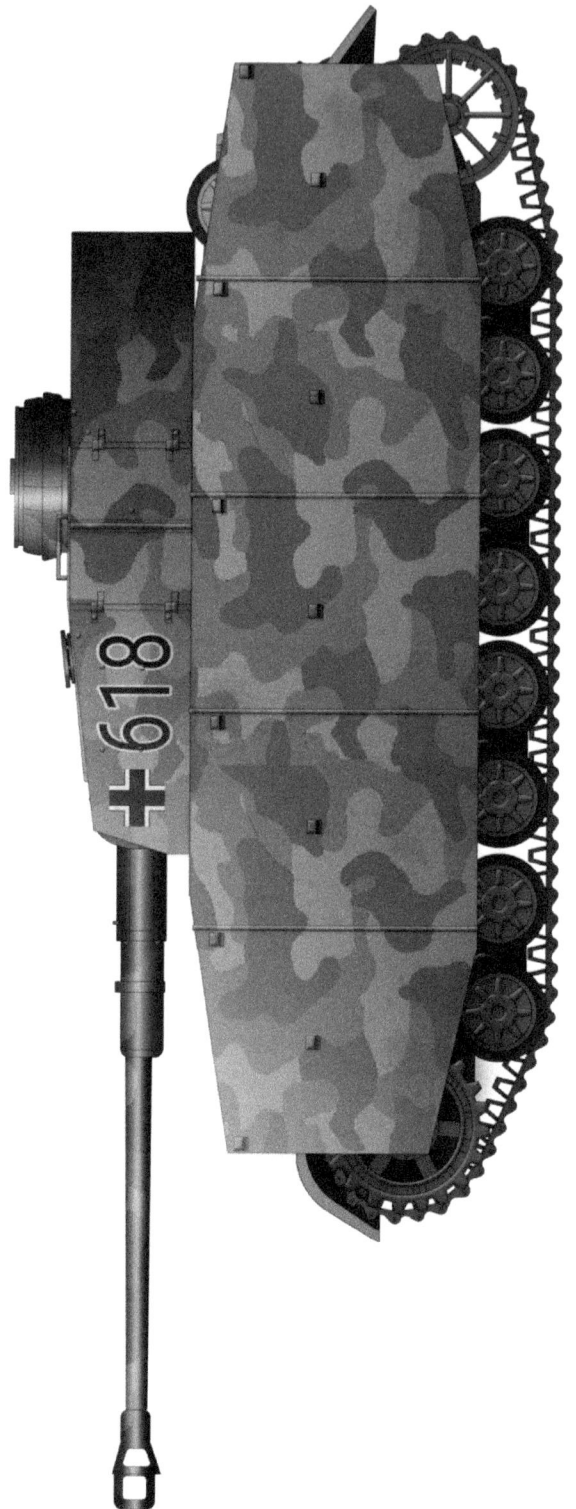

PzKpfw IV Ausf. H (Sd.Kfz. 161-2), SS-Pz.Rgt. 1, SS-Pz.Gren. Div. "LSSAH", Milan, Italy, september 1943

Moravia, where the unit was to be transformed into a division. Among the new units was the *Abteilung 'Schönberger,'* still under the orders of the *SS-Stubaf.* Schönberger, created from the 'tracked' units of the heavy battalion: the assault guns of the *4.(Stug.)Kp.*, passed to the orders of *SS-Ostuf.* Emil Wiesemann[5] and the *Marder I* tank fighters of the *Panzerjäger-Kompanie (Sfl.).*

SS-Stubaf. Schönberger.

One of the first examples of *StuG.III* Ausf. B in training.

A *StuG.III* and *LSSAH* soldiers on the streets of Mariupol.

A *Leibstandarte* assault cannon inside Taganrog.

Eastern Front

The *Leibstandarte*'s assault guns participated in the summer of 1941 in the invasion of Soviet territory, distinguishing themselves in the course of fighting for the annihilation of the Uman pocket in July 1941, then at Melitopol in September, and at Mariupol and Taganrog during October. Just after the capture of Taganrog with the units marching in the direction of Rostov, on October 26, the *II./LSSAH* launched an attack to try to take enemy positions: it was only thanks to the support of the *Leibstandarte*'s assault guns, that the *7.Kp./LSSAH* of *SS-Hstuf.* Sandig, managed to penetrate the Soviet lines south of the Tschaptschach Gorge, catching two enemy companies by surprise, which surrendered en masse. On October 28, the Soviets again attacked the positions of the *II./LSSAH*, but were once again repulsed thanks in part to the intervention of Emil Wiesemann's assault guns.

Soldiers and *Leibstandarte* assault cannon during The fighting in Taganrog (NARA).

A *StuG.III* of the *LSSAH* on its way to Rostov, 1941.

Later, the assault guns of the *Leibstandarte Adolf Hitler* were hard at work in the fighting to take Rostov-on-Don in November 1941. In particular, the platoon of four *StuG IIIs*, under the orders of *SS-Ustuf.* Georg Isecke, capable of resolving several critical situations in relief of other German units, along with the *11.Kp./LSSAH* under the orders of *SS-Ostuf.* Joachim Peiper and a few tanks of *Panzer-Regiment 4*. In early December, the *Abteilung 'Schönberger'* was engaged to cover the units' retreat to the Mius line, where the division remained throughout the winter in a defensive position, repelling Soviet attacks until the spring of 1942. On December 26, 1941, *SS-Sturmbannführer* Georg Schönberger was decorated with the German Cross in Gold for the outstanding field leadership of his armored unit.

Leibstandarte Panzers 1940-1945

A *Leibstandarte* assault gun in combat in the Rostov area, 1941.

Soldiers and *StuG.III* of the *LSSAH* near the Rostov station.

Notes

(1) For the complete history of the unit, read the complete divisional history of the *Leibstandarte* in two volumes by the same author. See Bibliography.

(2) The adjective *Verstärkte* (reinforced) did not please Commander Sepp Dietrich, who on September 5, 1940, ordered that it no longer be used.

(3) Georg Schönberger, was born on February 21, 1911 in Munich, SS-Nr. 1 351. After attending the *SS-Junkerschule* in Bad Tölz, he was assigned to the *Leibstandarte*. In April 1936, thanks to the availability of some armored cars, he was placed under the orders of a motorized platoon.

(4) For Michael Wittman's complete biography and military career, read the book written by the author himself. See Bibliography.

(5) Emil Wiesemann, born September 11, 1914, Berlin, SS-Nr. 54 514 He entered the *Stabswache* on July 8, 1933. After a course at the infantry school in Döberitz, he served as platoon commander in a machine gun company. From February 1940 he was sent to the *SS-Junkerschule* in Braunschweig, becoming *SS-Ustuf.* in the *SS-StuG.-Batterie 'LSSAH'*. During the Balkan campaign he distinguished himself at the head of the assault gun platoon, receiving the Iron Cross Second Class. On May 7, 1941, he was promoted to *SS-Obersturmführer*.

Leibstandarte Panzers 1940-1945

Stug III Ausf.B (Sd.Kfz.142)(7.5 cm StuK L-24) Russia winter 1941/42

Leibstandarte Panzers 1940-1945

StuG III Ausf.D at Mariupol (Ukraine). 1941

II) The armored regiment

On May 15, 1942, the OKW Operations Command transmitted the *Führer*'s new orders regarding the reorganization of the *LSSAH* already in the Mariupol sector and the establishment of a motorized *Waffen SS* Army Corps, which was to comprise the first three SS divisions. Between June 1 and July 2, the *Leibstandarte* divisions were put to rest in the Mariupol sector, in reserve to the *1.Panzer-Division*. On July 10, 1942, the order finally came to transfer to the Western Front, where Hitler feared a possible British landing on the Atlantic coast. *The Leibstandarte* divisions were therefore transferred to the area east of Paris. The transfer of the SS divisions to France was part of German plans to reorganize the first three SS divisions, *Leibstandarte*, *Das Reich* and *Totenkopf*, into new *Panzergrenadierdivisionen* of the *Waffen SS*, with the addition of an armored division for each unit, as well as a heavy company equipped with the new *Tiger* tanks. While still on the Eastern Front, the division immediately began the formation of new divisions for the unit's new structure and motorization.

One of the new *StuG.III Ausf F* assigned to the division, 1942.

Schönberger and Dietrich.

Iron Crosses to members of the *SS-StuG.-Abt. 'LSSAH'* (NA).

In particular, the *SS-Abteilung 'Schönberger'* was to be transformed into a new assault gun group, the SS-Sturmgeschütz-Abteilung 'LSSAH' with two new batteries formed as early as March 1, 1942. The new unit thus comprised a total of three batteries, each with seven *StuG.IIIs*. At the same time, the staff of the General Staff of the former *'Schönberger' Abteilung*

Stug III F Abt 191 Eastern front during the test. 1942

served as a nucleus for both the formation of the new divisional armored unit and the assault gun group itself.

To provide the missing manpower for *the I.Panzer-Abteilung*, the former *SS-Panzer-Abteilung 'LSSAH'*, *SS-Stubaf*. Schoenberger transferred the cadres and personnel of the assault guns he knew very well. And so the commander of *the SS-Stutmgeschütz-Abteilung 'LSSAH,'* the *SS-Stubaf*. Max Wünsche, left his unit along with many officers and some very experienced men. In the photo, taken in the spring of 1942 on the Russian front, *SS-Ogruf*. Sepp Dietrich with officers of the *Leibstandarte* assault gun unit including Heinz von Westernhagen, Emil Wiesemann, Max Wünsche and Karl Rettlinger (*Bundesarchiv Bild 101III-Gayk-006-07A*).

SS-Ostuf. Ralf Tiemann.

Formation of the Panzer-Abteilung

As early as February 1942, while *LSSAH* units were still on the Eastern Front, the formation of an armored battalion for the *Leibstandarte* had begun at Camp Wildflecken. The official formation order was dated January 24, 1942. Personnel were recruited from within the unit itself but also from other reinforcement and training units and initially regrouped at Lichterfelde. *SS-Panzer-Abteilung 1* was initially placed under the orders of *SS-Stubaf*. Wilhelm Mohnke, replaced as early as February 20, 1942, by *SS-Stubaf*. Schönberger. The unit was to be structured on three companies and a command company. In command of the *1.Pz.Kompanie* was placed *SS-Hstuf*. Manfred Schmidt, of the *2.Pz.Kompanie, SS-Ostuf*. Ludwig Lamprecht, of the

Leibstandarte Panzers 1940-1945

Sepp Dietrich and the *SS-Hstuf.* Max Wünsche, spring 1942.

Summer 1942: Some *PzKpfw.IV Ausf.* F2 of the *3.Pz.Kp.* in training in France, in the Paris area. In the foreground *is SS-Stubaf.* Georg Schönberger.

More *Pzkpfw.IV Ausf* F2 of the *2.Pz.Kp.* in training.

3.Pz.Kp., the *SS-Ostuf.* Ralf Tiemann. The armored companies were equipped with *PzKpfw IV* tanks with short 75mm cannon, but also included light platoons equipped with *PzKpfw II* tanks. On April 13, the units were transferred to complete training, to the Sennelager camp near Paderborn in Westphalia. On June 13, 1942, the *1.Zug* of the *3.Pz.Kp.* was equipped with new *PzKpfw IV F2* with 75mm L43 cannon. The *2.Zug* of the same company remained with its *Pz IVs* with short 75mm L24 cannon. On June 20, after a visit by *SS-Ogruf.* Dietrich and a training session with live ammunition, the battalion's formation was deemed completed, so the unit was ready for transfer to the Eastern Front. Its transfer to the Melitopol area was short-lived, however, as all *Leibstandarte* units, from mid-July were transferred to France. The *SS-Pz.Abt. 1*, in particular, to the Melun area, south of Paris. On July 29, the armored units of the *Leibstandarte* paraded through Paris, ahead of von Rundstedt, Hausser and Dietrich. The next day, they reached their new destination, the pioneer barracks in Evreux, where instruction of the wards resumed. On October 10, *SS-Pz.Abt. 1* left Evreux to move to the Orbec sector, twenty kilometers southwest of Lisieux: the wards quartered in the castle of Mervilly. On October 14, the *SS-FHA* issued the order for the formation of a second armored battalion for the *Leibstandarte,* as part of the creation of an entire armored regiment. The command of the regiment was assigned to the *SS-Stubaf* himself. Georg Schönberger.

PzKpfw.IV Ausf. F2 of *3.Pz.Kp.* in training in France, Paris area, summer 1942.

SS-Ustuf. Georg Isecke.

The establishment of the second battalion led to numerous changes in the command of the various departments: for example, the commander of *3.Pz.Kp.*, *SS-Ostuf.* Ralf Tiemann, became regimental adjutant (*Regimentsadjutant*) and his company passed to *SS-Ostuf.* Waldemar Schütz. The new battalion was formed with elements of *SS-StuG.Abt.1* in the Evreux barracks. *SS-Stubaf.* Max Wünsche, until then commander of the latter unit, assumed command of the battalion (*I.Abteilung*), designating as his adjutant *SS-Ustuf.* Georg Isecke. It was planned to structure the battalion on three medium companies (*mittleren Panzerkompanien*) with each company consisting of a *leichter Zug* (light platoon) with four *Pzkpfw III Ausf L* (*Sd.Kfz.141*) and two *mittlere züge* (medium platoons) with four *PzKpfw IV* (*Sd.Kfz.161*) each. The command of the *1.Pz.Kp.* was given to *SS-Hstuf.* Arnold Jürgensen, the *2.Pz.Kp.* to *SS-Ostuf.* Wilhelm Beck and the *3.Pz.Kp.* to *the SS-Hstuf.* Ludwig Lamprecht. The former *SS-Pz.Abt. 1*, thus became the *II./SS-Pz.Rgt.1* under the orders of *SS-Stubaf.* Martin Gross: its three existing *Panzerkompanien*, were renumbered, thus becoming the *5., 6.* and *7.Pz.Kp.* In command of the *5.Pz.Kp.* remained the *SS-Hstuf.* Manfred Schmidt, the *6.Pz.Kp.* was succeeded by the

Leibstandarte Panzers 1940-1945

SS-Stubaf. Martin Gross.

SS-Hstuf. Heinz Kling.

SS-Ostuf. Hans Pfeiffer and at *the 7.Pz.Kp.*, the *SS-Ostuf.* Waldemar Schütz. Following the arrangements for the new structure of the three *mittleren Panzerkompanien* of *II./SS-Pz.Rgt.1*, each of which was to include one *leichter Zug* on *PzKpfw III* and two *mittlere Züge* on *PzKpfw IV*, the light platoons equipped with *Panzer II Ausf. F* were detached from the companies and transferred to the staffs of the two battalions and the regiment. In addition, the six short-gun *PzKpfw IV Kwk 75s* still in the *7.Pz.Kp.* were transferred to a German police unit.

The Schwere Kompanie

As part of the formation of the first SS armored corps, the formation of a heavy armored battalion, equipped with the new *Tiger* tanks, was also planned at the Fallingbostel camp in the fall of 1942. All three SS divisions, *Leibstandarte*, *Das Reich* and *Totenkopf*, provided personnel. Eventually, however, battalion formation was postponed because of the lack of sufficient *Tiger* tanks, so it was decided to assign at least one *Tiger* company to each of the three divisions. The heavy company for the *Leibstandarte*, placed under the orders of *SS-Hstuf.* Heinz Kling, was formed and trained always in Fallingbostel. Personnel were taken not only from the *Panzer Regiment* of the *LAH*, but also from the assault gun group. The *schwere Kompanie* of *SS-Panzer Regiment 1*, comprised three heavy platoons, equipped with four *Tiger* tanks each and one light platoon, equipped with five *Pzkpfw III* tanks. The company included a total of 306 men, officers, non-commissioned officers and troops, with a vehicle fleet of 119 vehicles, including tanks. As Kling's aide, there *was SS-Ostuf.* Waldemar Schütz, who, during the training phase, was in command of the company's first platoon. The second platoon, on the other hand, was under the orders of *SS-Ustuf.* Hannes Philipsen, while the third was under the orders of *SS-Ustuf.* Helmuth Wendorff. The light platoon, equipped with five *Pzkfw III* tanks, was assigned to *SS-Ustuf.* Michael Wittmann: after being decorated with the Iron Cross First Class in September 1941 and promoted to *Oberscharführer*, Wittmann had been sent to attend the course for aspiring officers at the SS academy in Bad Tölz. The main task of Wittmann's light platoon was to protect the *Tigers* from short-range attacks from enemy anti-tank or infantry units. Offensive operations were secondary; the platoon was to serve as a defensive screen for the *Tigers*.

Tiger tank crews during a training session, fall 1942.

SS-Ustuf. Michael Wittmann.

The *Panzer IIIs* were armed with the 50mm long gun with protective reinforcement plates at the hull and turret. Wittmann's tank had the identification number (*Turmnummer*) '4L1'. Commanding the other tanks were *SS-Oscha.* Max Marten (4L2), the *SS-Uscha.* Franz Staudegger (4L3), *SS-Scharführer* Georg Lötzsch (4L4) and *SS-Unterscharführer* Schwerin (4L5).

Departmental training and formation

On October 20, 1942, *SS-Stubaf.* Schoenberger was officially placed in command of the *Panzer-Regiment 'LSSAH'*. The three company commanders of the *I./SS-Pz.Rgt. 'LSSAH'*, *SS-Hstuf.* Arnold Jürgensen, *SS-Hstuf.* Lamprecht and *SS-Ostuf.* Wilhelm Beck, participated in a special course for company commanders that began on Nov. 2 at the Army *Panzertruppen-Schule* in Wünsdorf and ended on Dec. 7. On Nov. 22, the *SS-Division (mot.) 'Leibstandarte SS Adolf Hitler'* officially became the *SS-Panzer-Grenadier-Division 'Leibstandarte SS Adolf Hitler.'* The training of armored units continued apace, particularly in the ranks of the *I.Panzer-Abteilung* of the *SS-Stubaf.* Wünsche, which had been formed later and whose personnel still had to familiarize themselves with the new materials and doctrines of employment. The *SS-Hstuf.* Heinz Kling officially assumed command of the *4.(schwere) Panzer-Kompanie* on Dec. 24 although he had held this post since Dec. 2. Beginning Dec. 20, a number of *Bordführer* (tank commanders) and *Fahrer* (tank drivers) were sent to the *Henschel-und Wegmannwerk* factory in Cassel for technical training.

A first-generation *Tiger* tank fresh out of the factory and ready for battle.

On December 30, 1942, the *SS-Panzer-Korps* and *SS-Panzer-Grenadier-Division 'LSSAH'* were ordered to the Donetz sector on the Eastern Front. The tankers of *SS-Panzer-Regiment 'Leibstandarte'* were to receive their full winter equipment and prepare their vehicles for deployment in Russia. For the *4.(schwere) Kp.*, its 10 *Tigers* and 15 *Panzer IIIs* were delivered to it only on Jan. 21, 1943: 3 examples of each model were assigned per platoon. Consequently, training could only begin intensively in Fallingbostel from this date, with platoon-level exercises. On January 30, 1943, it was the turn of the *SS-Panzer-Regiment 'LSSAH'* repair platoon to leave Fallingbostel for the Eastern Front. Initially, Hitler had planned to use the *SS-Panzer-Korps* for the counteroffensive that was to enable the liberation of the surrounded *6.Armee* at Stalingrad, but the lack of sufficient trains for the transfer of the *'Leibstandarte SS Adolf Hitler'* and *'Das Reich'* divisions as well as the operational unavailability of the *Totenkopf*, which needed further weeks of training to which was later added the capitulation of Paulus's army. As a result, the *Führer* decided to commit the two first SS divisions to the defense of the city of Kharkov, now threatened by the Red Army, pending the *Totenkopf*.

Leibstandarte Panzers 1940-1945

Panzer III Ausf J Leibstandarte a Karkov 1943

III) On the Kharkov Front

The transfer of the *SS-Panzer-Regiment 'Leibstandarte'* took place in several stages, some tanks were still to be recovered in Burg, near Magdeburg. And so, the *7.Kompanie* surrendered short-gun *Panzer IVs* in exchange for 6 *Panzer IV Ausf. F2* painted white. For its part, the *Tiger-Kompanie* began to be loaded at Fallingbostel in three convoys (Jan. 31, Feb. 1 and 2, 1943) for transfer to the Eastern Front: the heavy tanks were unloaded at Kharkov from Feb. 7. While the *Leibstandarte* continued to deploy its units in the sector assigned to the *SS-Panzer-Korps* of *SS-Ogruf.* Paul Hausser, all Soviet assaults were repulsed between the Kotomlia and Annovka positions.

German *Panzers* and grenadiers marching through the snow in the area east of Kharkov, February 1943.

A *PzKpfw III Ausf M* from the *Leibstandarte* at Poltava.

On Feb. 9, it was decided to shorten the defensive front to allow the SS Armored Corps to form a *Stossgruppe*, an assault group, at Merefa. The *I./SS-Pz.Rgt. 'LSSAH'* of the *SS-Stubaf.* Wünsche was at that time the only armored unit with the full complement available. But as the last *Panzer-Regiment* convoys disembarked their men and materiel, not all the tanks were sent to the front, as some were sent to the rear. In fact, after being delayed at Stargard due to a tank fire, the last convoy of the *4.(schwere)/SS-Pz.Rgt. 'LSSAH'*, carrying 6 *Tigers* and 3 *Panzer IIIs*, under the command of *SS-Ustuf.* Wittmann on Feb. 9, after being unloaded was sent to Poltava where it remained near the station until March 6, without receiving any operational employment!

Men and vehicles of *Kampfgruppe Meyer* of the *Leibstandarte* ready to attack, February 1943.

The *PzKpfw.IV '205'* of the *2.Kp./SS-Pz.Rgt. 'LSSAH'* (C. Trang).

On February 10, the *SS-Pz.Rgt. 'LAH'* integrated into the *SS-Pz.Korps Stossgruppe*, was split into three *Kampfgruppen*. The *Kampfgruppe 'Meyer'*, under the orders of *SS-Stubaf.* Kurt Meyer was the most powerful formation, comprising the *SS-Panzer-Aufklärungs-Abteilung 'LSSAH'*, Wünsche's *I./SS-Pz.Rgt.* and the latter regiment's *6.Kompanie* under the orders of *SS-Ostuf.* Hans Astegher. This grouping was to make an 85-kilometer arc movement from Novaia Vodolaga to Alexeievka. In the center of the device, *Kampfgruppe 'Kumm'* was to capture the position of Ochotchaie, with the *5.* and *7.Panzer-Kompanien* remaining under the

Leibstandarte Panzers 1940-1945

Panzer III ausf M SS Liebstandarte Ukrain 1943

command of *SS-Stubaf.* Martin Gross. The next day, this grouping met strong enemy resistance, while elements of the *II.Abteilung* remained pinned down in front of the Borki station. *Kampfgruppe 'Meyer'* was able to attack from Merefa and penetrated several tens of kilometers inside the Soviet lines.

Some vehicles of *Kampfgruppe Meyer* engaged in opening fire against a Soviet defensive position. Kurt Meyer himself, taking cover behind *Panzer '216'* directs fire against the enemy resistance nest (*Charles Trang Collection*).

Maintenance of a *Tiger* tank on the Kharkov front, 1943.

Out of the five Tigers engaged in combat, two were lost due to mechanical problems, and a third disappeared into a stream after a bridge collapsed under the weight of its 54 tons. On Feb. 12, motorcyclists from *'Das Reich,'* supported by several tanks of the *II./SS-Pz.Rgt. 'LSSAH,'* pushed the Soviets back from Novaia Vodolaga after six hours of fighting. *SS-Ostuf.* Rudolf von Ribbentrop was wounded during renewed fighting during the evening and refused to board the *Fieseler Fi 156* Storch that was to evacuate him to the rear. The next day, the *Panzer-Regiment* announced the number of operational tanks: 12 *Panzer II*, 12 *Panzer III* and 41 *Panzer IV*. On Feb. 14, Wünsche's *I./SS-Pz.Rgt. 'LSSAH'* attacked from Jefremovka, pushed all the way to Alexeievka and established liaison with the *SS-Stubaf.* Kurt Meyer.

Leibstandarte Panzers 1940-1945

SS-Ostuf. Rudolf von Ribbentrop on his *Panzer IV Lang* during the fighting for Kharkov. Despite being wounded, he decided to return immediately to the command of the 7.*Panzer-Kompanie* (*Bundesarchiv*).

Elements of *the 1./SS-Pz.Rgt. 'LSSAH'* of the *SS-Hstuf.* Jürgensen, with *Panzer IV Ausf. F2 '128'* in the foreground followed by other tanks (NARA).

German *Panzers* and grenadiers on the snowy steppe, 1943. *'LSSAH'* lost 3 *Panzers*.

The Soviet 6th Guard Cavalry Corps, grouped in the Paraskoveia-Ochotchaie-Bereka triangle, was annihilated in the fighting that followed. Despite this tactical success, the situation was still not favorable to the Germans: in fact it became even more critical. Hausser's *SS-Panzer-Korps* had received an explicit order from Hitler: "*Defend Kharkov at all costs! If necessary, stand in a defensive position.*" But the pressure from the Soviet units was too great, and to persist in defending the city to the bitter end would have caused the SS units to be encircled and led to their safe and unnecessary annihilation. The Soviet encirclement maneuver was imminent and elements were already attacking the western outskirts of the city. *SS-Ogruf.* Hausser therefore requested permission to evacuate Kharkov, but was not granted. Ignoring *the Führerbefehl* (Hitler's order), the SS-General disobeyed and ordered, at 4:45 p.m., the retreat of his units, *Leibstandarte, Das Reich* and *Grossdeutschland*, in the direction of the Udy River. The next day, 9 *Tigers* of the *4.(schwere)/SS-Pz.Rgt. 'LAH'*, left Kharkov following Hausser's retreat directives to intervene on Alexeievna, then stationed in Krasnograd for technical maintenance. On Feb. 16, 1943, fighting raged ahead of Ochotchaie and the *II./SS-Pz.Rgt.*

Leibstandarte Panzers 1940-1945

SS-Ostuf. Walter Malchow.

SS-Ostuf. Wilhelm Beck.

SS-Ustuf. Walter Malchow, of the *5.Panzer-Kompanie*, distinguished himself and the four *Panzer IVs* of his platoon with an 80-kilometer raid inside the Soviet lines. He thus succeeded in destroying numerous anti-tank pieces, and his report on enemy positions was crucial to the continuation of operations. On February 17, 1943, *SS-Ostuf.* Beck distinguished himself at the head of his *2.Panzer-Kompanie*, which often found itself in the vanguard of *Kampfgruppe Meyer*. On February 19, the *Panzer-Regiment* had 12 *Panzer IIs*, 10 *Panzer IIIs*, 45 *Panzer IVs* and 21 *Befehlspanzers*. The following day, the *I./SS-Pz.Rgt. 'LSSAH'* stood in a defensive position at Jeremeievka. On Feb. 21, Meyer and Wünsche attacked southward together: their units destroyed or captured 19 76.2-mm guns, 4 45-mm anti-tank guns and 7 heavy mortars, in addition to inflicting heavy losses on Soviet infantry. On that same day, the *Panzer-Regiment* had 49 *Panzer IVs* and 6 *Tigers* as operatives. On Feb. 23, *Kampfgruppe Meyer* attacked Paraskoveievskie capturing or destroying another 20 76.2 mm guns, 4 122 mm howitzers, 3 100 mm guns and 3 rocket launchers. The Soviet divisions that managed to penetrate south of Ordivka were contained thanks to the intervention of Martin Gross's *II./SS-Pz.Rgt. 'LSSAH'*. *SS-Ostuf.* Hans Astegher, commander of the *6.Panzer-Kompanie* particularly distinguished himself during these battles by closing a breach opened by the Soviets in the Novaia Vadolaga sector, allowing them to preserve the bridge over the Vilkhuvatka River, vital for the retreat of the entire *SS-Panzer-Korps*. The next day, *II./SS-Panzer-Grenadier-Regiment 1* counterattacked on Bulachi with *SS-Stubaf* tanks. Martin Gross: 5 *T-34s*, 7 guns, 5 heavy mortars and between 400 and 500 *Frontoviki* (Soviet soldiers) were knocked out. On February 25, the general retreat of the *Leibstandarte* was associated with some new violent counterattacks. That of Max Wünsche's *I./SS-Pz.Rgt.* launched from Losovaia toward the west inflicted major losses on the enemy forces: 37 76.2 mm guns, 10 45 mm guns, 6 122 mm howitzers, one captured German howitzer (*s.FH 18*), between 300 and 400 animal-drawn vans, and about 800 casualties, but no prisoners were taken. On February 26, the fighting shifted to the Krasnograd sector, where *SS-Hstuf.* Schmidt, who until then had remained in reserve with his *5.Panzer-Kompanie*, had to launch an attack against a Soviet anti-tank front.

A *PzKpfw.III* engaged on the Kharkov front, February 1943 (NARA).

A *PzKpfw.IV* engaged in combat, February 1943.

He destroyed 19 anti-tank guns out of the 24 identified, then continued on to Olchovatka with only 5 *Panzer IVs* and a company of grenadiers. After numerous hours of fighting at least 9 *T-34s*, 4 antitank guns, 2 trucks, 14 tows, 300 Soviet infantrymen killed, as well as a captured *Panzer III* taken back from the enemy were claimed as destroyed. After a few days, the combined efforts of the *1.* and *4.Panzer-Armee* led to the annihilation of the Soviet 6ªArmy and Popov grouping, which had pushed too far between German positions. Taking advantage of this serious mistake by the *Stavka* (the Soviet General Staff), the Germans counterattacked starting on February 19, first between Slaviansk and Novaia Vodolaga, then over the entire extension of the front as far as Bjelgorod. On March 2, the *Leibstandarte* thus participated in the *SS-Panzer-Korps* offensive. The connection with the 'Das Reich' division was established at Paraskoveia, and *Kampfgruppe Meyer* captured the Kegitchevka position. Thus, a pocket was formed around Jeremeievka, where numerous Soviet rifle divisions were trapped within it.

The *PzKpfw.IV '205'* of the *2.Kp./SS-Pz.Rgt. 'LSSAH'* passes through a Ukrainian village (C. T.).

SS-*Ustuf.* Rudolf von Ribbentrop.

By February 3, the *Leibstandarte* had destroyed 101 enemy tanks. On March 3, *Kampfgruppe Meyer* established liaison with *Totenkopf* Division at Jeremeievka, closing the pocket around the Soviet forces that had been forming for several days. On that same March 3, *SS-Ostuf.* von Ribbentrop, having just completed his convalescence, was placed at the head of the *7./SS-Pz.Rgt. 'LSSAH,'* thus becoming the fifth commander of this unit since the beginning of operations. This demonstrated the high number of losses suffered by the SS armored units.

The reconquest of Kharkov

Aggregated with *I./SS-Pz.Rgt. 'LSSAH'*, the *4.(schwere) Panzer-Kompanie* was moved 30 kilometers north of Krasnograd. Several Tiger tanks complained of mechanical problems before they were even engaged in combat, such as that of *SS-Uscha.* Brandt, which fell victim to engine overheating and was permanently lost, destroyed by fire. Committed to the vanguard of *the 4.Panzer-Armee* for the decisive counteroffensive toward Kharkov, the *SS-Panzer-Korps* was deployed at the connection point between the latter army and the *Armee-Abteilung 'Kempf'* and went on the attack on March 6 with the *Totenkopf* behind the *Leibstandarte* on the left and *Das Reich* on the right.

Leibstandarte Panzers 1940-1945

A Tiger engaged on the Kharkov front, March 1943.

A Tiger of the *4.Kp./SS-Pz.Rgt. 'LSSAH'* passes a newly destroyed Soviet anti-tank piece, March 1943.

The Tigers marched with the *Panzers* of the *SS-Stubaf.* Wünsche in the direction of Walki and clashed with a *Pakfront* near Blagodatnoie. The Soviet defensive line was penetrated, but immediately T-34s successfully opposed the *Panzers* and an already damaged Tiger was immobilized, while that of *SS-Ustuf.* Helmut Wendorff sank into the Msha River, whose ice surface, though thick, could not withstand the weight of the heavy tank. The next day, *Kampfgruppe Meyer*, again supported by Wünsche's *I./SS-Pz.Rgt. 'LSSAH'*, captured the key position of Walki by attacking from the west. The *2.Panzer-Kompanie* under the orders of *SS-Ostuf.* Beck still distinguished himself leading the attack, but his losses were heavy: 3 *Panzers* were destroyed by shots from Soviet anti-tank pieces, including that of the *SS-Oscha*. Hans Reimling, decorated with the Knight's Cross three days later after falling in combat aboard his tank. He was promoted to the rank of *SS-Untersturmführer* posthumously.

SS-Oscha. Hans Reimling.

A *PzKpfw.III* on the march during the recapture of Kharkov.

Leibstandarte Panzers 1940-1945

PzKpfw IV Ausf J SS Leibstandarte in Francia 1942

On March 8, the attack continued in the Ljubotin sector. Towards evening, the *II./SS-Pz.Rgt. 'LSSAH'*, supporting *SS-Pz.Gren.Rgt.1*, announced the destruction of 5 *T-34s* and 30 guns.

PzKpfw.IV '615' of the 6.Kp./SS-Pz.Rgt. 'LSSAH' on the march, March 1943.

The German counteroffensive made important progress, particularly in the SS units' sector: Korotitch, 10 kilometers from Kharkov, was captured and a bridgehead was established on the Udy River. The next day, *Kampfgruppe Meyer* launched a new raid of about sixty kilometers, capturing in succession the positions of Peressetchnaia, Dergatchi, Tcherkaskoie and Zirkuny, 10 kilometers northeast of Kharkov!

Grenadiers and Panzers of the Leibstandarte on the outskirts of Kharkov, 1943.

Threatened with being surrounded, the city was to be captured by March 11. Hausser's plan was as follows: the *Leibstandarte* was to attack from the north and *Das Reich* from the west. The first *Panzers* to reach the Kharkov suburbs were Wünsche's. A *KV-1*, hidden behind a house, managed to destroy several German tanks, among them the *Panzer IV '727'* of the *SS-Ustuf*. Luis Stollmayer, who died in the flames of his tank.

Kampfgruppe Witt tanks penetrate inside Kharkov, March 1943.

Grenadiers of *Kampfgruppe Hansen* and *PzKpfw.IV* '728' inside Kharkov.

One of the four Tigers that supported the attack against the city took the lead to open the march. A duel with another *KV-1* followed: a shell from the latter hit the Tiger's optics, the pointer was killed and *SS-Ustuf*. Johannes Philipsen was wounded. Despite the loss of this vehicle, the momentum of the *Leibstandarte* and its *Panzers* did not stop.

Ammunition loading aboard a Tiger tank, March 1943.

At least 6 more *T-34s* were destroyed in ten minutes and by the end of the evening, the road was open to the Red Square of the Ukrainian city. The last suburbs of Kharkov were captured on March 14, and the roundups in the city continued until the next day.

Grenadiers and *PzKpfw IV* of the *Leibstandarte* on the outskirts of Kharkov.

The conquest of Bjelgorod

Column of *PzKpfw IV* advancing on the Ukrainian front, 1943.

Column of *Kampfgruppe Peiper* marches toward Bjelgorod.

SS-Stubaf. Martin Gross aboard his tank.

On March 16, some tanks of the *5./SS-Pz.Rgt. 'LSSAH'* supported the attack on Dementeievka. The Soviet forces, defeated at Kharkov, fell back toward Bjelgorod. On the 17th, another assault in the direction of this location was launched with the support of *SS-Ostuf*. von Ribbentrop's *7.Panzer-Kompanie*. Three *Panzer IIIs* and 1 *Tiger* aggregated with *Kampfgruppe Peiper* destroyed five tanks and a Soviet anti-tank piece. On March 18, two Tigers supported the *III.(gep.)/SS-Pz.Gren.Rgt.2 of the SS-Stubaf*. Joachim Peiper and penetrated the first enemy defensive lines and continued toward Bjelgorod. Towards evening, 14 tanks, 16 guns, 14 anti-tank guns, 52 machine guns and 38 trucks were destroyed, while on the German side they complained of only one casualty and six wounded. The next day, an armored group, with elements of the *7./SS-Pz.Rgt. 'LSSAH'* and 2 Tigers, including that of *SS-Hstuf*. Kling, received orders to re-establish links with the *Pz.Grenadier-Division* 'Grossdeutschland'. The tanks were near Strelezkoie, northeast of Bjelgorod, and destroyed 2 *T-34* and 1 *KV-2*, 2 76.2mm anti-tank guns, 1 reconnaissance armor, and 1 152mm gun. *SS-Stubaf*. Martin Gross distinguished himself again during these last battles for Bjelgorod. Leading his battalion in his *Befehlspanzer III '555'*, he was the first to enter the town despite numerous enemy anti-tank guns: thirty-two of them were destroyed or captured.

Leibstandarte Panzers 1940-1945

PzKpfw IV Ausf. SS Leibstandarte Division,
Zitadelle 1943

IV) Reorganization of departments

Fighting continued north of Bjelgorod until March 26, 1943, but mud and poor weather conditions made any attempt to exploit the important tactical success of Paul Hausser's *SS-Panzer-Korps* impossible. In fact, despite the loss of Kharkov and Bjelgorod, the Soviets had retained the bulk of their forces and had established an important salient around the city of Kursk that represented a dangerous wedge between the German lines, which absolutely had to be eliminated.

Crew members of a Tiger engaged in maintenance, spring 1943.

SS-Stubaf. Georg Schönberger delivers a decoration, under the gaze of Max Wünsche.

From March 25, most of the *Leibstandarte Tigers* were regrouped in the northern suburbs of Kharkov. After *Leibstandarte Adolf Hitler* withdrew from the front line on March 27, 1943, his *Panzer-Kompanien* were equally put to rest in the Kharkov sector. The units had to carry out technical maintenance on the vehicles, since in the previous fighting most of the vehicles had been put through their paces.

Leibstandarte Panzers 1940-1945

General Guderian, visiting the *Pz.Rgt.* of the *Leibstandarte*, examines the Tiger '405'. On the right, *SS-Hstuf.* Hans Kling.

The *SS-Pz.Rgt 'LSSAH'* was to be reconstituted and reorganized, especially after the departure for Germany of the *I.Abteilung* of the *SS-Stubaf.* Max Wünsche, which was to be re-equipped with the new *Panther* tanks. The *SS-Stubaf.* Gross took advantage of this and recovered *Panzers III* and *IV* to recomplete the ranks of his *II.Abteilung*, as well as the *Panzer IIs* liberated after the departure of the *Stabs-Kompanie*. Changes also occurred in the chain of command of the *SS-Stubaf* regiment. Schönberger. *SS-Ostuf.* von Ribbentrop exchanged his post at the head of the *7.Kompanie* with *SS-Hstuf.* Ralf Tiemann, *Regimentsadjutant*. The *SS-Hstuf.* Hans Pfeiffer, had taken charge of the *6.Kompanie* after Astegher's serious wounding, as well as that of the commander of his 1st platoon, *SS-Ostuf.* Ludwig Ruckdeschel. Recruits from *the Luftwaffe*, Göring's famous 'gifts,' completed the units. The next weeks of instruction were intensive to train them in the rudiments of the *Panzerwaffe*. The *SS-FHA* had ordered, as of March 23, the three *schwere Panzer-Kompanien* of the *Waffen-SS* to be reorganized according to *K.St.N.1176e* issued on March 5, 1943: it was planned to equip three platoons with 4 *Tigers* with a *Kompanie-Trupp* of 2 *Tigers* (1 *Tiger* for the *Kompaniechef* and a second replacement). The *4.(schwere)/SS-Pz.Rgt. 'LSSAH'* was therefore reorganized into three platoons of 4 *Panzer VIs*. The surplus *Panzer IIIs*, were ceded to the other units of the *I.Abteilung*. At the beginning of April, *Generaloberst* Heinz Guderian made an inspection in the *Panzer-Regiment 'LSSAH'* barracks. At the same time, it was ordered to reorganize the regiment according to the new tables (*K.St.N.1175a* of 25/01/1943). Each *Panzer-Abteilung* was to comprise four *mittlere Panzer-Kompanien* each with 22 *Panzer IVs*. The *I.Abteilung* having returned to Germany to recover its *Panthers*, only the *II.Abteilung* of the *SS-Stubaf.* Gross was subjected to this restructuring. The light platoon on *Panzer II Ausf. F* was equally assigned to the *Regiments-Stab*. Eventually, several regimental companies were renumbered, the *Panzer-Pionier-Kompanie* was renamed as *9.(Pionier)/SS-Pz.Rgt. 'LSSAH'*. In early May, the *4.(schwere)/Panzer-Kompanie* became the *13.schwere Panzer-Kompanie*. So new *Turmnummers* were painted on its tanks. By the end of May, only 7 *Tigers* were operational at the company's base in Olchany. On June 29, the *Leibstandarte* began to leave the Kharkov sector. The next day, *SS-Panzer-Regiment 'LSSAH'* had 12 operational *Panzer IIIs* out of the theoretical 13 (1 was under repair), 63 operational *Panzer IVs* out of the theoretical 87 (3 under repair) and 11 *Panzer VI Tigers* out of the theoretical 14 (2 under repair). Note that the regiment always had some *Panzer IIs* within the two *leichte Panzer-Kolonnen*.

V) Operation Zitadelle

On July 1, 1943, the *SS-Panzer-Grenadier-Division 'LSSAH'* received its attack orders from Hausser's *II.SS-Panzer-Korps* as part of Operation *'Zitadelle'*. The next day, his *Panzer-Regiment* obtained a new supply of vehicles, with 16 *Panzer IVs* and 5 *Panzer VI Tigers*. These new vehicles formed a material reserve for the *Panzer-Kompanien* for the future offensive. By July 4, 12 operational *Tigers* were stationed south of the Tomarovka-Bykovka road near elevation 222.3, then moved into the area east of Yakovlevo. On July 5, Operation *Zitadelle* began with a violent artillery barrage, 11 *Tigers* launched against the 220.5 elevation under the orders of *SS-Hstuf*. Kling.

Grenadiers and Tigers of the *Leibstandarte* waiting to go on the attack, July 1943 (NARA).

Tiger tanks and grenadiers of the *Leibstandarte* in the Kursk area.

Some Soviet defensive positions were destroyed without complaining of losses, while other positions were allowed to be overrun and then pulled against the most vulnerable parts of the German heavy tanks. The high ground was eventually captured and the *Tiger* tanks continued on to Bykovka, a position that was captured around noon.

Leibstandarte Panzers 1940-1945

SS-Hstuf. **Heinz Kling (NARA).**

SS-Ustuf. **Michael Wittmann (BA).**

The Soviets had suffered heavy losses, lost numerous anti-tank guns, and *T-34* carcasses were burning on the battlefield. The *Tiger '1305'* of *SS-Hstuf.* Kling with its pointer, the *SS-Strm.* Warmbrunn, had managed to destroy in the course of the day at least 9 flamethrowers, 7 *bunkers*, 4 *T-34s* and 19 7.62 mm anti-tank guns. For his part, *SS-Ustuf.* Michael Wittmann had destroyed 8 tanks and 7 anti-tank guns, then his *Tiger '1331'* was hit and immobilized.

The next day, with two more *Panzer VIs*, *SS-Hstuf.* Kling captured elevation 243.2 east of Yakovlevo. At 1:15 p.m., the Soviets launched an attack supported by 38 tanks from this very location. The *Tigers* participated in the German counterattack, destroying 8 more tanks, and continued their march, retaking the lead of the armored grouping with a view to conquering the heights west of Prokhorovka. *SS-Hstuf.* Schmidt, commander of the *5./SS-Pz.Rgt. 'LSSAH'*, distinguished himself equally during these last battles: while leading the armored grouping, he spotted between 40 and 50 Soviet tanks in the Yakovlevo valley. Taking up a position on high ground, he managed to destroy, with only 3 *Panzer IVs*, at least 11 *T-34s* and 6 anti-tank guns. Over the course of the last two days, Kling's unit claimed the destruction of 50 *T-34s*, 1 *KV-1*, 1 *KV-2* and 43 anti-tank pieces. At the head of the armored formations, *the Tigers* had perfectly fulfilled their role as breaking means, but the tanks, heavily stressed and exposed to all obstacles, suffered major losses. And so it was that Sepp Dietrich ordered that the damaged *Tiger* of *SS-Uscha.* Brandt be disassembled to recover spare parts for the repair shop. During the night, the fighting continued. Attempting a penetration inside Teterevino, 3 *T-34s* were destroyed by a *Tiger*. On July 7, violent fighting occurred at Lutchki and Teterevino: enemy armored counterattacks were repulsed, but Dietrich's division's progression was slowed considerably. At the end of the day, the *7.Panzer-Kompanie* of the *SS-Hstuf.* Tiemann, nevertheless claimed the destruction of 43 *T-34s*! The armored groups (*Panzergruppen*) of the *Leibstandarte* and *Das Reich* continued to advance in parallel along the Teterevino-Prokhorovka road. Since the beginning of the offensive, Units of the *SS-Panzer-Grenadier-*

Division 'LSSAH' had destroyed 75 tanks and 23 guns, as well as shot down 12 Soviet planes.

Tiger '1311' of the *Leibstandarte* Heavy Armored Company during a break in the fighting on the front south of Kursk, July 1943.

SS-Uscha. Franz Staudegger.

On July 8, the *SS-Panzer-Regiment 'Leibstandarte'* clashed with a number of Soviet armored formations, comprising a total of about 40 tanks, in the Rylsky sector. The *SS-Ostuf.* Malchow distinguished himself in his *Panzer IV '515'* by destroying numerous *T-34s*. The attack of the *II./SS-Pz.Rgt.'Leibstandarte'* was later blocked by a massive anti-tank front, which was soon bypassed by four Tigers under the orders of *SS-Hstuf.* Kling. Numerous buried enemy tanks were put out of action. At 6:15 p.m., a new danger loomed when the *Panzergruppe* reported by radio that a Soviet brigade had penetrated its lines east of elevation 252. Two Tiger heavy tanks were present in this sector, including '1322' commanded by *SS-Uscha.* Staudegger with the damaged rolling train. The *Tigerkommandant* somehow managed to move the vehicle by getting immediately in front of the enemy armored formation. He spotted the Soviet tanks halted, in tight formation, in a small valley. A formidable target. Staudegger destroyed 17 of them, then five more as the Soviets retreated, a total of 22 in less than two hours. The *SS-Uscha.* Staudegger had to fall back, however, due to lack of ammunition. For this action, he received the Knight's Cross on July 10, 1943. During that same day, the *Tiger-Kompanie* of the *Leibstandarte* destroyed 42 *T-34* tanks and 3 *General Lee* tanks.

Tiger '1313' of *13.(schw.)Kp./SS-Pz.Rgt.1* during a break in the fighting, July 1943.

The *PzKpfw.IV* of *SS-Ostuf.* von Ribbentrop.

While clashes between the mechanized formations continued between July 9 and 10, the divisional *Panzergruppe* led an attack on July 11 against Soviet positions on the northern slope of elevation 252.2, crossed the anti-tank ditch and occupied the southern slope soon after. The three Tigers, including that of *SS-Hstuf.* Kling, supporting the attack against the hill claimed the destruction of 28 anti-tank guns and six howitzers. During the same engagement, seven *Panzer IVs* of the *6./SS-Pz.Rgt. 'LSSAH'* were engaged in battle: the '604' tank of *SS-Ostuf.* Rudolf von Ribbentrop managed to destroy at least one enemy tank. *SS-Ostuf.* Walter Malchow of the 5.*Kompanie*, distinguished itself again, destroying 7 more Soviet tanks. But the *Panzergruppe*'s flanks remained uncovered and the Prokhorovka road had not yet been opened. At that time, *SS-Panzer-Regiment 'LSSAH'* lined up 4 *Panzer IIs*, 5 *Panzer IIIs*, 47 *Panzer IVs* and 4 operational *Panzer VIs*. On July 12, at 9 a.m., the Soviets launched a new attack against the *Panzergruppe* moving with 35 tanks from Prokhorovka and another 40 tanks from Petrovka. The Soviet tanks marched at full speed, backed by massive fire from their artillery.

SS-Stubaf. Martin Gross (BA).

SS-Rttf. Hans Siptrott.

Aboard his '604', *SS-Ostuf.* von Ribbentrop was in position with 6 other *Panzer IVs* of his *6./SS-Pz.Rgt. 'LSSAH'* and had their fire open at about 250 meters distance. Visibility was not optimal due to dust raised by the movement of the tanks, smoke from the firing and black clouds rising from the burning tanks. Some tank duels took place at a distance of 10 to 30 meters. Rudolf von Ribbentrop personally destroyed 14 *T-34s* with his '604', the *SS-Hstuf.* Schmidt claimed 36 with his *5.Panzer-Kompanie*, while *SS-Uscha.* Hans Siptrott, of the *7.Kompanie*, destroyed 6 alone. The *II./SS-Pz.Rgt. 'LSSAH'* of the *SS-Stubaf.* Gross claimed a total of 62 *T-70* and *T-34* tanks were destroyed, to which another 25 were added during a second Soviet attack. Martin Gross and Rudolf von Ribbentrop were decorated with the *Ritterkreuz* for their actions. Despite these local tactical successes, the Soviets continued to fight by committing numerous armored units and with massive artillery support, succeeding in blocking the Germans.

The *Leibstandarte* managed to hold the positions gained the day before, but its advance in the direction of Prokhorovka was completely blocked. On July 13, the *Panzergruppe* continued its advance, but continued to meet strong resistance from the Soviets. The next day, the *SS-Panzer-Regiment 'Leibstandarte'* lined up 4 *Pz.Kpfw.II*, 6 *Pz.Kpfw.III*, 32 *Pz.Kpfw.IV* and 5 *Pz.Kpfw.VI 'Tiger'* operatives. According to a staff report, the division destroyed or captured 501 Soviet tanks in the period between July 5 and 14, 1943. On July 15, *Panzergruppe 'Leibstandarte'*, comprising the *II./SS-Pz.Rgt. 'LSSAH'*, *II./SS-Art.Rgt. 'LSSAH'* and elements of *III./SS-Pz.Gren.Rgt.2*, reached the sector located east of Ivanovka amidst a thousand difficulties. At that time, fifty tanks were still operational within the division: 4 *Panzer II*, 6 *Panzer III*, 32 *Panzer IV*, 8 *Tiger*. The next day, thanks to the work of the mechanics of the repair shop, another 10 tanks were refitted.

Leibstandarte Panzers 1940-1945

Leibstandarte tanks engaged in combat on the Ukrainian steppe. On the left and in the center, note some burning Soviet tank carcasses, July 1943.

A German armored column on the Ukrainian front, July 1943.

However, on July 17, Adolf Hitler ordered the retreat of the *II.SS-Panzer-Korps* from the Kursk battlefield and ordered the cessation of Operation *'Zitadelle'* because of the Allied landing in Sicily: the *Leibstandarte Adolf Hitler*'s units were to regroup in the area west of Bjelgorod. Beginning on July 24, the transfer of the divisions by train began. On July 27, the SS Division officially received the transfer order for Italy. *SS-Panzer-Regiment 'LSSAH'* had to surrender all its operational tanks to *SS-Panzer-Regiment 'Das Reich'* and *Totenkopf*, which were to be engaged on the Mius front.

Leibstandarte Panzers 1940-1945

PzKpfw IV Ausf. F2 URSS 1943

VI) Reorganization in Italy

The first elements of the *SS-Panzer-Regiment 'LSSAH'* arrived in Innsbruck, Austria, on August 5, 1943, to be then headed for Parma and Reggio. The only *Panzers* available were those that had not been surrendered by the unit, despite orders received. The regiment's *Stabs-Kompanie* had in fact retained all its vehicles. Fortunately, new supplies had been planned, and on August 7, crews from the *II.Abteilung* picked up new *Panzer IVs* at Parma and Reggio stations. On August 9, the *7.Pz.Kp.* of *SS-Hstuf.* Tiemann received 22 new *Panzer IVs* at Modena.

SS-Pz.Rgt.1 staff vehicles in Innsbruck, 1943 (*Horst Schumann Collection*).

SS-Hstuf. Kling signs documents in front of a Tiger.

In general, the *Leibstandarte's* equipment increased considerably. In fact, the next day, the *I.Abteilung* of the *SS-Stubaf.* Kuhlmann arrived by train in the Parma-Reggio sector, coming directly from Grafenwöhr, where it had been equipped and trained on *Panther* tanks: the *1., 2., 3.* and *4.Panzer-Kompanien* were each equipped with 17 *Panther Ausf. D* and the *Stabs-Kompanie* had 3 *Befehlspanthers*. The *I./SS-Pz.Rgt. 'LSSAH'* was a new unit that had little to do with Max Wünsche's previous battalion that had distinguished itself in the fighting at Kharkov. Barely a third of the manpower came from the latter; most of the cadre came from the SS armored units' depot and instruction unit and from the ranks of the *SS-Sturmgeschütz-Abteilung 'LSSAH,'* which had already provided a large part of the initial contingent. Kuhlmann himself, the *Abteilungkommandeur*, did not come from the *Leibstandarte*. He had previously been in command of the *I./SS-Pz.Rgt. 'Das Reich,'* which he had left in April 1943.

SS-Ostubaf. Georg Schönberger, second from right, discusses the situation with other officers of *I./SS-Pz.Rgt.1* at a location in Italy in the summer of 1943 in front of a *Panzer*. Second from the left is *SS-Stubaf*. Herbert Kuhlmann.

Tigers of the *Leibstandarte* on the Italian front, summer 1943.

The commander of the 1.*Panzer-Kompanie* was *SS-Hstuf*. Werner Pötschke, former commander of *1./SS-Aufkl.-Abteilung 2*, the 2. was under the orders of *SS-Ostuf*. Hans Stübing, a *StuG* veteran of the *Leibstandarte*, while 3. and 4. were under the orders of *SS-Ostuf*. Kurt Kleist and *SS-Ostuf*. Ernst Otto, who came from the infantry ranks. Twenty-seven new *Tiger I Ausf*. E arrived at Reggio station between August 10 and 13, including two *Befehlstiger*. On August 25, the *SS-Hstuf*. Kling reached *Tiger-Kompanie* after a period of convalescence. The *13.(schwere)/SS-Pz.Rgt. 'LSSAH'* was then temporarily placed under the orders of *SS-Ustuf*. Helmut Wendorff, while a part of the effectives with also some new recruits was allocated

Pz.IV of II./SS-Pz.Rgt.1 on the streets of Milan, September 1943.

to form a *Tiger-Abteilung* within the *I.SS-Panzer-Korps* (the future schwere *SS-Panzer-Abteilung 101*) under the orders of the same *SS-Hstuf.* Heinz Kling.

On Sept. 7, *SS-Pz.Rgt. 'LSSAH'* reported 3 *Panzer II*, 5 *Panzer III*, 51 *Panzer IV*, 65 *Panzer V Panther* and 23 *Panzer VI Tiger* as operational, while there were still 1 *Panzer II*, 1 *Panzer III*, 3 *Panzer IV*, 6 *Panzer V* and 4 *Panzer VI* under repair. Two days later, operational tanks were 3 *Panzer II*, 6 *Panzer III*, 53 *Panzer IV*, 66 *Panther* and 23 Tiger. On that same September 9, *Leibstandarte* units were ordered to position themselves in front of the Italian garrisons in the sector to obtain their disarmament. The occupation of Milan was entrusted to the *II.Abteilung*. The tank drivers of the *I.Abteilung* encountered numerous mechanical problems with their *Panthers*. Every move or exercise ended in fires, breakdowns and other engine failures, creating considerable problems for the repair shop. To such an extent, that on October 21, all *Panthers* of the *I./SS-Pz.Rgt. 'LSSAH'* were loaded onto rail platforms to reach the Army arsenal depot in Burg (Magdeburg-Königsborn). These vehicles, which had been delivered between June and July 1943, were qualified as *'nicht frontverwendungsfähig,'* meaning 'unusable for combat.' The tanks were to be rechecked and undergo modifications at the *Demag* workshops in Falkensee. On October 22, the *SS-Panzer-Grenadier-Division 'Leibstandarte SS Adolf Hitler'* became, by order of the *SS-FHA*, the *1.SS-Panzer-Division 'Leibstandarte SS Adolf Hitler'*. As a result, the armored regiment officially became *SS-Panzer-Regiment 1 'LSSAH'*. On October 27, some Tiger personnel equally went to the Burg depot to pick up Tiger tanks to take them to the unit. At the same time, *Panther* crews took charge of 34 new vehicles on October 30, then 41 the next day. On November 1, 1943, 21 additional tanks were delivered, and this new supply brought the total to 96 tanks received instead of the 71 returned. This also allowed the unit to be able to form a fourth platoon of 5 *Panthers* in each *Panzer-Kompanie*. As far as the *Abteilungs-Stab* was concerned, it recovered three *Panthers* with which it was possible to form a reconnaissance platoon (*Aufklärungs-Zug*) on *Panther* with five other tanks.

VII) Return to the Eastern Front

In the meantime, the *Leibstandarte* had received orders to move to the

Eastern Front to deal with the critical situation in Ukraine. Only the *Panzer-Kompanien* of *II./SS-Pz.Rgt.1* were operational at that time and could be sent to the front with the rest of the division. Convoys with *Panthers* arrived in stages a few days later in the Berditchev sector. Trains carrying Tigers recovered in Burg reached Lemberg (Lviv) on November 2, but were eventually diverted to Paderborn on direct orders from the *SS-FHA*. With the sudden departure for Ukraine, the *13.(schwere) Panzer-Kompanie* had been organized on five platoons, each on five Tigers, plus two more Tigers from the *Kompanie-Trupp* (for the *Kompaniechef* and the *Kompanietruppführer*). *The Leibstandarte* was assigned to the *XLVIII.Panzer-Korps* of *General der Panzertruppen* Hermann Balck, who had been ordered, after the fall of Kiev on November 6, to launch a counteroffensive toward the Ukrainian capital with a series of successive attacks on Brusilov, Zithomir and Fastov.

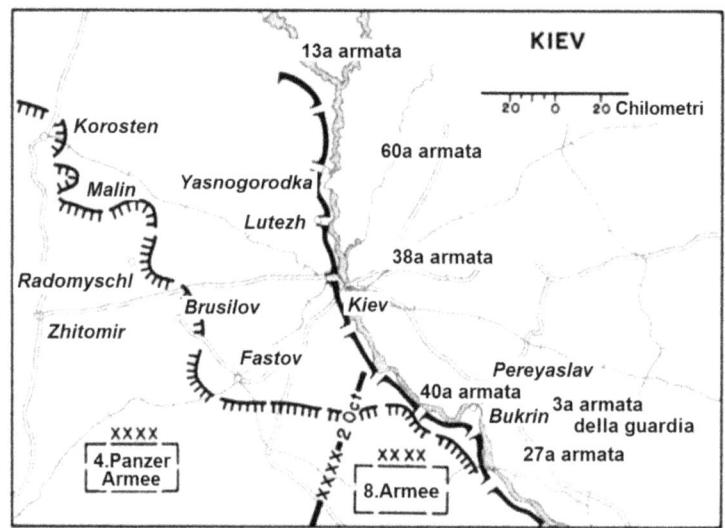

The Ukrainian front between October and November 1943.

SS-Stubaf. Kuhlmann.

A PzKpfw.IV with infantry on board, November 1943.

The SS Division was to counterattack in the direction of the latter town, on the southern flank of the Soviet advance. On November 8, the first units of *SS-Pz.Rgt.1* began arriving at Berditchev station. The companies immediately set out separately, with the roads turned into huge quagmires by the autumn rains.

Leibstandarte Panzers 1940-1945

Panther column on the move in Ukraine, November 1943.

The next day, of the *I.Abteilung*, there were only the *Stab* of the *SS-Stubaf.* Kuhlmann and the equivalent of a *Panther-Kompanie* that had arrived directly from Burg. The *Panthers* had to be painted white, with paint applied to the *Zimmerit*. Tactical numbers still had to be painted on the turrets. A *Kampfgruppe* 'Kuhlmann,' comprising 22 operational *Panthers*, two grenadier companies and a pioneer company on half-tracks, went on the attack the next day on Popielnia. The muddy terrain slowed the progression and caused the tanks to consume large amounts of fuel. At about 9 p.m., Kuhlmann reported that his attack had been repulsed. He then had to fall back on Kamionka and urgently called for a refueling.

Panther of I./SS-Pz.Rgt.1 of the *Leibstandarte* marching on the Ukrainian front, November 1943.

Panther and half-tracks waiting to move to attack.

On November 11, the starting positions for the counteroffensive were reached after violent fighting. The *SS-Stubaf.* Kuhlmann renewed his attack on Popielnia, which he succeeded in capturing around 9:30 a.m. after destroying four enemy tanks. The army corps ordered him

51

German Panther G 1943

to make a flanking movement northeast of the location. The SS officer then received orders to occupy high ground located west of Fastov, about 25 kilometers from the town. Around noon, the *Kampfgruppe* reached the forests near the objective, then was to reach Kornin after first refueling its tanks.

A column of *PzKpfw.IV* during an attack, November 1943.

SS-Oscha. **Konrad Heubeck.**

On Nov. 13, *Kampfgruppe 'Kuhlmann'* established liaison with the armored elements of the *1.Panzer-Division* at Balki, then fought inside Kornin facing Soviet tanks and an infantry battalion, which were put to flight after a hard fight. On November 15, *I./SS-Pz.Rgt.1* was moved north of Solovievka. The *2.Panzer-Kompanie* of *SS-Ostuf.* Hans Stübing claimed the destruction of 12 *T-34s*, 1 *T-70* and 10 anti-tank guns. *SS-Oscha.* Konrad Heubeck particularly distinguished himself during the latter fighting. The *XLVIII.Panzer-Korps* later decided to attack northward from the Kornin sector, aiming to cut the Kiev-Zithomir road in order to hit the Soviet units from behind. The attack succeeded and caught the forces of the 1st Ukrainian Front by surprise: the position of Solovievka and other important localities fell into the hands of the SS units. On November 17, the *II./SS-Pz.Rgt.1* of the *SS-Stubaf.* Gross attacked from the latter location to the northeast, then turned to cut off the enemy rear. The Lutchine position was overrun by infantry elements supported by 10 *Tigers* of the *13.(schwere)/SS-Pz.Rgt.1*, which destroyed five *T-34s* in an hour of hard fighting. The next day, the Soviets counterattacked in force.

Panzer and elements of the *Leibstandarte* reconnaissance group, November 1943.

SS-Ostubaf. Georg Schönberger.

Kampfgruppe 'Kling', with its *Tigers*, was forced to retreat westward, then resumed its positions the next day after destroying 4 more *T-34s*. Meanwhile, German forces were advancing; Zithomir was captured by the *1st* and *7.Panzer-Division*. It was now necessary to annihilate the Soviet forces clustered around Brusilov. But the Soviets launched numerous attacks to reopen the Kiev-Zithomir road. On November 20, the commander of *SS-Pz.Rgt.1*, *SS-Ostubaf.* Schoenberger, was killed around noon by shrapnel during a bombardment of his command post in Soloviëvka. He was decorated with the Knight's Cross posthumously. The *Divisionkommandeur* of the *Leibstandarte*, *SS-Oberführer* Theodor Wisch, replaced him with *SS-Sturmbannführer* Joachim Peiper, commander of *III.(gep.)/SS-Pz.Gren.Rgt.2*. A designation that aroused much astonishment, since Himmler's former aide-de-camp had never served in the armored divisions, nor had he undergone trai-

Leibstandarte Panzers 1940-1945

SS-Sturmbannführer **Joachim Peiper.**

ning to command a regiment! And so, while the divisions of the *XLVIII.Panzer-Korps* reported tactical successes, such as the *19.Panzer-Division* that penetrated enemy lines and established a link with the *1.Panzer-Division* east of Brusilov, the *Leibstandarte* units were slowed down by numerous Soviet defensive positions established around the various locations to be overcome. In the end, the Soviets thus succeeded in blocking the offensive of Adolf Hitler's personal guard, which, for the first time since the beginning of the war, failed to accomplish its mission! On November 23, *SS-Panzer-Regiment 1* reported 23 *Panzer IVs*, 15 *Panthers* and 4 *Tigers* operational. *Kampfgruppe 'Kraas'* went on the attack in the direction of Lasarovka, but the *Panzers* in the vanguard, including that of *SS-Oscha*. Siptrott (7.Pz.Kp.) were hard engaged in Dubrovka. *Panzergruppe 'Peiper'* invested the position, then captured the village of Lasarovka with momentum, while *I./SS-Pz.Rgt.1* was stranded along the Privorotïe-Divin road.

Leibstandarte tiger during a difficult march through Ukrainian mud.

On November 24, *Panzergruppe 'Peiper'* attacked again, ending up against a *Pakfront* on the outskirts of Starizkaïa, while Soviet tanks attacked it on the flanks. Several *Panzers* were lost and 6 enemy tanks were destroyed. Jochen Peiper managed to reach the center of the locality, where the *SS-Oscha.* Hans Dauser, platoon commander in *the 2.Panzer-Kompanie*, distinguished himself with his *Panther*. *SS-Stubaf.* Jochen Peiper reported shortly afterwards that he was blocked in his progression in front of elevation 185.4.

A column of *Leibstandarte* Tiger tanks passes through a Ukrainian village, 1943.

A *Panther* of *SS-Pz.Rgt.1* on the march, November 1943.

New fights

On November 26, the thaw blocked all movement; Kiev did not fall and the Soviets reinforced in the area east of Brusilov. The *Leibstandarte* was to attack in the direction of Radomyschl the next day. On the 28th, *Kampfgruppe 'Kuhlmann'* (*I./SS-Pz.Rgt.1*) moved forward and hit the Soviet positions on the flank. At 2:00 p.m., the *Panther* established a link at Potachnaïa with the reconnaissance group of the *1.Panzer-Division*. *Kampfgruppe 'Peiper'*, with the rest of *SS-Panzer-Regiment 1* and *SS-Panzer-Aufklärungs-Abteilung 1*, moved south of Radomyschl, then turned on Garborov where it stood in a defensive position at the end of the day. The next day, *Kampfgruppe 'Peiper'* captured the latter location after an hour of fighting. In contrast, the *Leibstandarte* failed to capture Radomyschl.

Some *PzKpfw.IV* of *5./SS-Pz.Rgt.1* engaged in combat on the Ukrainian front. A *T-34* tank hit and pinned down is inspected by a *Waffen-SS* soldier, November 1943.

Between December 3 and 5, the *1.SS-Panzer-Division* reorganized its units. *SS-Panzer-Regiment 1* reported as operational 4 *Panzer III* (1 under repair), 30 *Panzer IV* (44 under repair), 28 *Panzer V* (52 under repair) and 4 *Panzer VI* (21 under repair).

A formation of *PzKpfw.IV* waiting to move to attack, November 1943.

The situation at the front continued to remain very critical, with the Soviet 60ªArmy threatening the left flank of Balck's *XLVIII.Panzer-Korps*. On December 6, German armored

Leibstandarte Panzers 1940-1945

Tiger I in panzergrau Russia 1943

corps forces crossed the Zithomir-Korosten road.

PzKpfw.IV engaged in combat, December 1943.

Styrty's position was captured by *Kampfgruppe 'Peiper'*, led by its commander with rapid assaults that surprised the Soviets because their development did not correspond to normal German tactics, being a mixture of infantry tactics and armored units. Peiper soon afterwards captured Tortchin and was pinned down west of Tchaikovka in front of an important *Pakfront. SS-Ustuf.* Wittmann distinguished himself in his Tiger, particularly during the penetration of this anti-tank line in front of Andreïev. However, *the Leibstandarte* regiment suffered new losses: the commander of 3./SS-Pz.Rgt.1, *SS-Ostuf.* Kurt Kleist, was killed at Sliptscizy along with one of his platoon commanders, *SS-Ustuf.* Friedl Tibcke. On December 7, *SS-Panzer-Regiment 1* was engaged south of Tchaikovka, but the *Panzers* were again blocked by an anti-tank front. *Panzer-Kampfgruppe 'Peiper'* diverted northward and captured Chodory. The *Panther* '201' of *SS-Ostuf.* Hans Stübing penetrated inside

A *Panther* with grenadiers on board during an attack.

Sabolot, but was hit by an anti-tank shell and caught fire. The SS-Officer managed to pull his shooter out of the burning turret, while he suffered severe burns. *SS-Ostuf.* Gerhard Scharke, commander of the *5.Panzer-Kompanie*, and *SS-Ostuf.* Herbert Sprunk, of the *7.Panzer-Kompanie*, were killed in the course of the fighting for Sabolot, which was captured on the morning of Dec. 8. *Panzer-Kampfgruppe 'Peiper'* destroyed or captured 1 T-34, 8 artillery pieces, 61 76.2 mm anti-tank guns, 1 45

Departments of *III.(gep.)/SS-Pz.Gr.Rgt.2* in a Ukrainian village, waiting to move to attack, December 1943.

A *T-34* tank hit by direct fire from a Tiger.

PzKpfw.IV engaged in combat, December 1943.

mm anti-tank gun, 21 anti-tank guns, 55 machine guns, 5 trucks. 930 Soviet soldiers were killed and only 3 prisoners were captured! On December 9, the *Leibstandarte*, blocked by strong Soviet resistance, suspended its attack northwest of Radomyschl. *SS-Panzer-Grenadier-Regiment 2* and *Panzer-Kampfgruppe 'Peiper'* were committed eastward for a new attack. The next day, Jochen Peiper executed a new raid southward, in the course of which he lost several *Panzers*, for failing to launch reconnaissance and underestimating the size of the enemy forces. As a result, *SS-Staf.* Teddy Wisch personally ordered him to stop his attack.

On December 14, 1943, *Panzergruppe 'Peiper'* diverted and overwhelmed Soviet forces along the Teterev River. The *Leibstandarte* pushed its advance until it came within about 3 kilometers of the Kiev-Korosten railway line. On December 18, the division attacked Meleni having the Korosten road as its target. The next day, *SS-Panzer-Regiment 1* reported as operational 33 *Panzer IV*, 12 *Panzer V*, 7 *Panzer VI*. By the end of the day, *Panzergruppe 'Peiper'* captured Peremoga, but was

A column of *PzKpfw.IV* marching on the Ukrainian front, 1943.

Tiger tanks engaged on the Ukrainian front, December 1943.

Grenadiers and *Panther* tank waiting to move to attack.

blocked 1.5 km to the east by a minefield and a new anti-tank front: *SS-Ostuf*'s *Panzer IV*. Malchow was destroyed and the SS officer was seriously wounded. Around midnight, Peiper's tanks were refueled on one side of the railroad embankment when a patrol spotted a Soviet armored unit intent on refueling itself, but on the other side of the embankment. Peiper then launched his *Panzers* forward in a surprise attack at night, succeeding in destroying several enemy tanks. Also present were some operational Tigers led by *SS-Ustuf*. Michael Wittmann, who had replaced *SS-Hstuf*. Kling, who had been called to command *II./SS-Pz.Rgt.1* to replace *SS-Stubaf*. Martin Gross who had been wounded. On Dec. 20, the *Leibstandarte* announced the destruction of 1,003 Soviet tanks since the beginning of the year. As of Dec. 21, the *Panzer-Regiment* reported 6 *Panzer IV*, 4 *Panzer V*, 2 *Panzer VI* as operational. *SS-Stubaf*. Joachim Peiper, who operated with his armored grouping in the Soviet rear, distinguished himself by his impressive deep raids in eliminating numerous defensive positions, but these actions were at the same time costly in terms of materials and personnel. Perhaps too costly in relation to the results achieved, since these tactical successes were often local and did not have such a decisive impact as to change the course of the fighting in general. In the division's officer corps alone, there were 13 casualties between Nov. 21 and Dec. 21, 1943, not counting the seriously wounded such as *SS-Ostuf.* Hans Stübing. And so Joachim Peiper was temporarily transferred to the divisional staff and the few operational tanks were placed under the command of *SS-Stubaf.* Kuhlmann. *SS-Panzer-Regiment 1* had few tanks at that time, having been literally decimated after a month of deployment to the front.

German armored formation on the Ukrainian front, December 1943.   Joachim Peiper.

An SS grenadier under cover of a *PzKpfw.IV*.

By the evening of Dec. 22, thanks to the work of the unit's mechanics, 12 *Panzer IVs*, 9 *Panthers* and 2 *Tigers* were operational. The next day, the *Leibstandarte Adolf Hitler* Armored Intervention Group, comprising 16 *Panzer IVs*, 7 *Panthers*, 3 *Tigers* and the remnants of *III.(gep.)/SS-Pz.Grenadier Regiment 2*, was engaged alongside the *291.Inf.Div.* to repel an armored attack. Four Soviet *T-34s* were destroyed in the course of the fighting.

The fights for Berditchev

On December 24, the remains of the *Leibstandarte* were moved south of Zithomir. A *Panzergruppe* under the orders of *Oberst* von Mellenthin, comprising 25 tanks under the command of *SS-Hstuf.* Kling, was engaged south of Chatrichtche.

Leibstandarte Panzers 1940-1945

SS-Ostuf. Helmut Wendorff.

SS-Ustuf. Michael Wittmann.

Grenadiers and *PzKpfw.IV* on the march.

On December 26, 12 *Panthers* of *I./SS-Pz.Rgt.1* managed to destroy 10 T-34s, complaining of the loss of only two tanks. The next day the SS division established a defensive line east of Berditchev. *Panthers* from the *I.Abteilung* together with some elements of *SS-Pz.Gren.Rgt.2* attacked toward Andruchevka, but were blocked at Ljassovka by a massive enemy barrage. On that day, 11 *Panzer IVs*, 13 *Panthers* and 5 Tigers were operational. By the 28th, the number of operational tanks was 17 *Panzer IVs*, 8 *Panthers* and 4 Tigers. The Soviets launched a massive attack with the aim of cutting the rail line to where supplies for the German forces engaged in this sector of the Dnepr passed. Regrouping at Tchubarovka, they were hit in the flank by 13 *Panther* which destroyed 8 *T-34s*. *SS-Ustuf.* Helmut Wendorff penetrated with some Tigers into the locality where he destroyed 11 more enemy tanks. The next day, he again distinguished himself by destroying 11 more Soviet tanks. In two days, Wendorff had destroyed 10 *T-34s* with his heavy tank, bringing the number of his total victories to 58! For his part, *SS-Hstuf.* Pötschke succeeded, at the head of a number of *Panthers*, in destroying numerous tanks and destroying 5 of the 35 T-34s advancing along the Zithomir-Berditchev railway line, lamenting the loss of only two *Panthers*. By December 31, 12 *Panzer IVs*, 7 *Panthers* and 2 *Tigers* were reported operational. On January 1, 1944, *Leibstandarte* tanks were engaged in only a few local operations, facing significantly superior enemy forces. Successes were achieved in each case: a single *Panther* in cover managed to destroy 4 of the 8 Soviet tanks that attacked along the Voliza-Trajanov road, while *SS-Ustuf.* Wendorff destroyed five more *T-34s*. Fighting multiplied in the front sector held by the division in the following days. On January 7, *SS-Stubaf.* Kuhlmann received orders to seize the enemy-occupied altitude 276.7, an important position from which the entire sector was overlooked: some *Panthers* managed to repel a Soviet attack, destroying 3 *T-34s*. At that time 6 *Panzer IVs*, 11 *Panzer Vs* and 2 *Panzer VIs* were operational. The next day, Kuhlmann again distinguished himself and his *Kampfgruppe* during a counterattack that enabled them to destroy 33 T-34s and 7 assault guns. On that occasion, *SS-Ustuf.* Michael Wittmann destroyed his 60th tank!

A Tiger tank under cover of a house, in ambush position, January 1944.

German grenadiers advance following a Tiger, 1944.

On January 9, the *Panther* destroyed 8 T-34s and 2 assault guns east of Cherebki. Two Tigers under the orders of Wittmann himself were launched to counterattack and destroyed another 12 *T-34s*, with the SS officer achieving his 66ᵃvictory: these new successes earned him a recommendation for the Knight's Cross. A few hours later, more *Panzer Vs*, held in reserve at Cherebki, destroyed 6 more Soviet tanks. On the 13th, some *Panzers* of the *Leibstandarte* were engaged as far as Tchesnovka, and in the course of the fighting 37 tanks and 7 assault guns were destroyed. At 11:20 p.m., the SS tanks were launched again on the counterattack with elements of *Kampfgruppe 'von Künsberg'* and *SS-Panzer-Grenadier-Regiment 1*: the front line was reestablished and Michael Wittmann alone claimed the destruction of 19 of the 37 *T-34s* destroyed! The ace had come to score 88 victories, 80 of them with the same shooter, *SS-Rottenführer* Balthasar Woll.

A Tiger engaged in combat on the Ukrainian front.

SS-Rttf. Balthasar Woll.

The next day, Wittmann received *the Ritterkreuz* from the hands of Commander Theodor Wisch, who had already proposed him the day before for the grant of the Oak Fronds! As for *SS-Rttf.* Woll, he in turn was decorated with the Knight's Cross on January 16, 1944. On January 14, *Panzer-Kampfgruppe 'Das Reich'* committed some of its tanks alongside those of the *Leibstandarte*, south of Molotchki. The next day, *SS-Panzer-Regiment 1* lined up 5 *Panzer IV*, 9 *Panzer V* and 5 *Panzer VI* as operatives. On January 16, *SS-Stubaf.* Kuhlmann managed to invest the southern outskirts of Krasnopol with 4 *Panther* supported by infantrymen of *SS-Pz.Gren.Rgt.2,*

January 1944: from left, *SS-Obf.* Wisch, 'Bobby' Woll and Wittmann after the ceremony to award the *Ritterkreuz*.

Leibstandarte Panzers 1940-1945

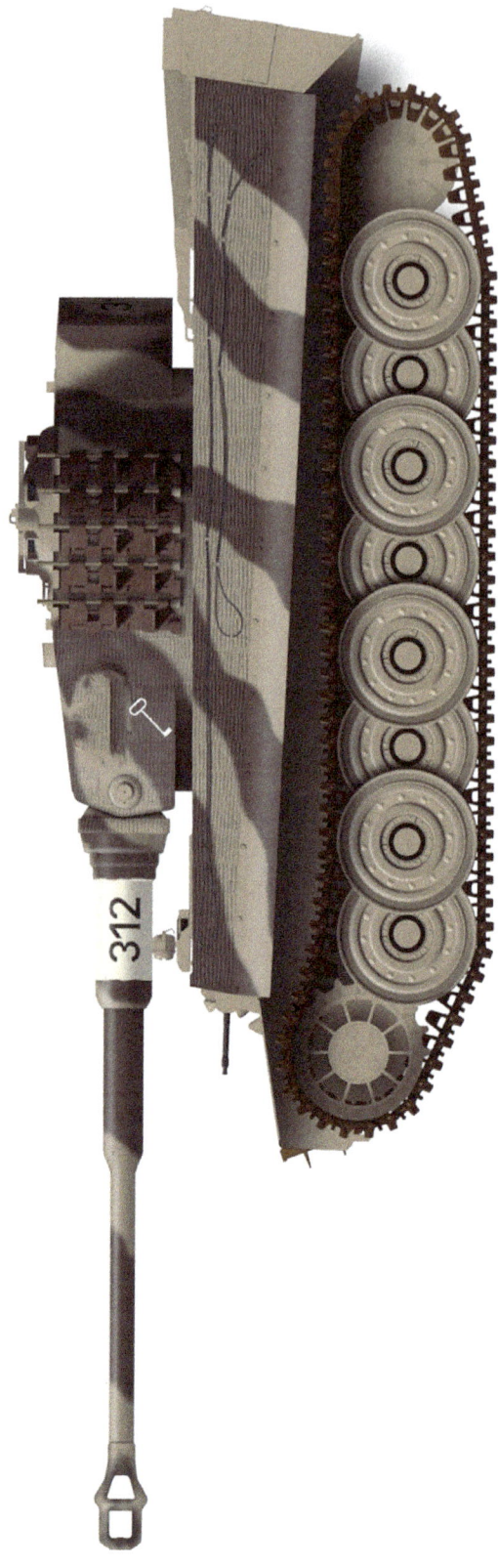

Tiger I in camouflage marking Russia 1943

destroying at least 6 enemy tanks during the attack. The next day, the *Panzergruppe* launched a new attack toward the center of Krasnopol, continuing to destroy numerous more enemy tanks. The *schwere Panzer-Kompanie* of *SS-Pz.Rgt.1* had managed to destroy 343 tanks, 8 assault guns, 255 antitank guns and 20 artillery pieces in 14 weeks of fighting and at least 146 tanks and 125 antitank guns between Dec. 5, 1943 to Jan. 17, 1944.

A column of *Panther* tanks of *I./SS-Pz.Rgt.1* marching on the Ukrainian front, January 1944 (*Trang*).

Tiger tanks marching on the Ukrainian front, January 1944.

For its part, *SS-Panzer-Regiment 1* would destroy 184 tanks of the 288 credited to the *Leibstandarte* between December 25, 1943 and January 18, 1944. *The Waffen-SS Tiger tanks had inflicted severe losses on the Red Army!*

Fighting East of Vinnitsa

The *Leibstandarte* was taken over between January 19 and 21, 1944. Its *Panzer-Regiment* lined up at that time 2 *Befehlspanzer IIIs*, 25 *Panzer IVs*, 22 *Panzer Vs* and 1 operational Tiger. On January 25, *Kampfgruppe 'Kuhlmann'* attacked Brizkoie, then marched on Otcheretnia. However, the SS units found strong Soviet resistance especially the next day near the 296.7 elevation. On the 27th, the *SS-Stubaf.* Kuhlmann, whose tanks were on the verge of running out of fuel, captured Lipovez station and stood in a defensive position. Some *Panthers* were able to fall back to the west after being resupplied. Kuhlmann's second, *SS-Ustuf.* Gottfried Winterhoff, was killed in combat on that day. By Jan. 25, *SS-Panzer-Regiment 1* was lining up 16 operational *Panzer IVs*, 9 *Panzer Vs* and 4 *Panzer VIs*. On January 28, 1944, *SS-Ustuf.* Michael Wittmann destroyed his 114th Soviet tank aboard his Tiger. The next day, *Kampfgruppe 'Kuhlmann'* was engaged in the capture of the Babin position.

PzKpfw.IV of 5.Kp./SS-Pz.Rgt.1 **engaged in combat, January 1944.**

A German armored formation engaged in the Korsun sector, 1944.

But in the meantime, the retreat of German forces at Berditchev had allowed the 1st Ukrainian Front to advance southward and create a pocket in the Korsun-Cerkassy sector, where some 58,000 German soldiers, grouped within *Gruppe 'Stemmermann'*, remained surrounded. Over the next few days, all German efforts were then concentrated on trying to break the Red Army's encirclement around the forces surrounded in this pocket. On January 30, *Kampfgruppe 'Kuhlmann'* was engaged in defending the Oratov station, while *SS-Ostuf.* Wittmann was decorated with Oak Fringes with as many as 117 enemy tanks destroyed to his credit. The next day, the *Leibstandarte* was finally taken over and transferred to the *III.Panzer-Korps* sector. The remnants *of II./SS-Pz.Rgt.1* arrived in the newly assigned area on February 3. At that time, *SS-Pz.Rgt.1* lined up 13 *Panzer IVs*, 11 *Panzer Vs* and 3 operational *Panzer VIs*. On Feb. 6, *Kampfgruppe 'Kuhlmann'* marched on Tinovka with 9 *Panther*, 2 Tiger with elements of *SS-Pz.Gren.Rgt.2*. The next day, it faced a dozen Soviet tanks, destroying seven of them. The *Kampfgruppe* was left with eight operational *Panthers* and Tigers.

Wittmann with Oak Fronds.

SS-Hstuf. Werner Pötschke.

On February 11, 3 *Panzer IVs* and 4 *Panzer Vs* remained operational. On the 15th, *SS-Ostuf.* Wendorff received the *Ritterkreuz*, and on February 17, it was the turn of the *SS-Stubaf.* Kuhlmann, as a reward for the achievements of his *Kampfgruppe* on the Ukrainian front. The *SS-Hstuf.* Kling, who had to his credit the destruction of 46 enemy tanks with his Tiger, received the *Ritterkreuz* in turn on Feb. 23, 1944.

On the Galician front

In early March, the *1.SS-Pz.Div. 'Leibstandarte'* was transferred to the dependencies of the *XLVIII.Panzer-Korps* deployed around Tarnopol. On March 3, the Soviets launched a massive offensive and penetrated the division's lines. The next day, a *Kampfgruppe*, comprising elements of various units and some tanks also under the command of *SS-Stubaf.* Kuhlmann, was launched into battle to fill the breaches. On March 6, *the Leibstandarte* was reinforced by the *schwere Panzer-Abteilung 503*, comprising 15 Tigers, which operated with the 11 *Panthers* and 6 Tigers of *SS-Pz.Rgt.1*. The German tanks covered the retreat of the other units, but complained of losses: by the evening of March 7, only 6 *Panthers* and 2 Tigers remained operational. In the rear, mechanics managed to refit numerous vehicles, and so by the next day 10 *Panthers* and 4 Tigers were operational. On March 9, *Leibstandarte* units were hard at work along the Gaidaika - Klininy line. A new *Panzergruppe* was then formed and Kuhlmann was ordered to open the main road to Manatchin. Aboard his *Panther*, *SS-Hstuf.* Pötschke launched a violent attack with 10 more *Panthers*, 4 Tigers plus 4 more Tigers from *s.Pz.Abt.503*: the village of Losova was captured and soon afterwards also the heights north of the same locality. Pötschke was later able to hold these positions despite subsequent enemy counterattacks. By the end of the evening, eight *Panzer Vs*, five *Panzer VIs* and four Tigers of *s.Pz.Abt.503* were operational. Between March 4 and 12, *Leibstandarte Adolf Hitler* had destroyed 35 *T-34s*, 3 KV-1s, 5 assault guns and 19 artillery pieces. But its losses had been equally high: by March 14, the division's *Panzer-*

Regiment was left with only 4 *Panther* and 2 Tiger, with 4 officers, 4 non-commissioned officers and 25 soldiers.

A Tiger of the *Leibstandarte*, March 1944.

German armored units overtake a convoy, March 1944.

As of April 1, the situation had not improved, and what was more serious, the *1.Panzer-Armee*, to which the *Leibstandarte* was aggregated, remained surrounded in the Kamenets-Podolsky pocket after a joint offensive by the 1st and 2nd Ukrainian Fronts. However, the *II.SS-Panzer-Korps*, comprising *the 9.SS-Pz.Div.* and *10.SS-Pz.Div.*, was transferred from France, succeeding in loosening the Soviet stranglehold at Buczacz, allowing the *1.Panzer-Armee* to fall back. *The Leibstandarte* was completely tried: after five months of continuous fighting and an exhausting retreat, the last members of *SS-Pz.Rgt.1* were attached to *Gruppe 'Balck'* on April 8. On the 12th, linkage was established with elements of the *'Frundsberg'* and the relief operation was completed. The last men of *SS-Pz.Rgt.1* engaged in Ukraine managed to reach the Brussels region.

VIII) On the Western front

As of April 25, 1944, the *1.SS-Pz.Div. 'Leibstandarte'* was subordinated to the *I.SS-Panzer-Korps* of *SS-Ogruf.* Josef Dietrich in Flanders. *SS-Panzer-Regiment 1* was quartered in the Hasselt sector. The reorganization of the regiment had been ordered in April 1944, according to the 'type 1943' structure, with two battalions out of four *Panzer-Kompanien* with 22 vehicles. But, at the beginning of 1944, the drastic decline in the production of armored vehicles by German industry could not guarantee the equipping of all units. The offensive potential of *SS-Panzer-Regiment 1* was thus greatly reduced in relation to its structure prior to its deployment in Ukraine.

Flanders, spring 1944: The *SS-Ostuf.* Fritz Steipart, hands out decorations to tankers of the *5.Kp./SS-Pz.Rgt.1*, who had distinguished themselves in earlier fighting (NARA).

SS-Ostubaf. Joachim Peiper, 1944.

The *Panzer-Kompanien* of the *I.Abteilung* thus had to be equipped with 17 *Panther* (three platoons of five vehicles) instead of the previous 22. For its part, the *II.Abteilung* remained equipped with 96 *Panzer IVs* (22 per company and eight for the staff and *Stabs-Kompanie*). The regiment also had to surrender its Tigers: the *schwere Panzer-Kompanie* was dissolved and its personnel transferred to the *schwere SS-Panzer-Abteilung 101*. Under these conditions, *SS-Ostubaf.* Joachim Peiper encountered considerable difficulties in getting his *Panzer-*

Regiment back on its feet. The tankers were trained as infantrymen waiting to receive their vehicles. In early May, *SS-Ustuf.* Reiser went to Mailly-le-Camp to recover 50 *Panzer V Panthers*. Despite the arrival of a large contingent of recruits from the *SS-Panzer-Ausbildung- und Ersatz-Regiment* in Riga, the personnel of *SS-Pz.Rgt.1* failed to reach 100 percent of its strength. In addition, the supply of tanks was still delayed.

A *PzKpfw.IV* of 7.Kp./SS-Pz.Rgt.1 during reorganization in Belgium, June 1944.

Joachim Peiper's *Befehlspanzer IV* (NARA).

In fact, individual instruction was possible only at the level of each crew post, with no battalion- or regimental-level exercises. As of June 1, 1944, *SS-Panzer-Regiment 1* had 42 operational *Panzer IVs* and 38 *Panthers*. Another 8 *Panzer IVs* were under repair. However, the *Leibstandarte* specified in a report dated June 4, 1944, that its armored regiment had only one operational company of 17 *Panzer Vs* and a second of 22 *Panzer IVs*, i.e., a quarter of its strength. Another convoys with materials arrived during June, when trains loaded with 33 and 20 *Panzer IVs*, respectively, left the depots on June 8 and June 17 bound for the Hasselt sector. Several other convoys loaded with *Panther* were destined for the *LSSAH* between June 14 and 29. In total, *SS-Panzer-Regiment 1* could have lined up 103 *Panzer IVs* and 72 *Panthers* in Normandy, with other vehicles arriving only during July.

Some armored vehicles of the *Leibstandarte* on the streets of Paris, June 1944.

A *Leibstandarte* tanker in Paris.

Transfer to Normandy

On June 6, 1944, the Allies landed in Normandy. Despite the fact that the *Leibstandarte* was not yet operational, the unit was put on alert, but did not move until the 9th, deployed east of Bruges, in reserve, south of the mouth of the Scheldt at the disposal of the *15.Armee*. Misled by Allied intelligence, the German high commands in fact believed that the real enemy landing would take place in the Calais Pass, while the one that took place in Normandy was only a diversion. In fact, the *Leibstandarte* did not receive its transfer order for Normandy until June 17, when the *Panzer-Regiment* was loaded onto platform cars. Rail traffic was severely hampered by Allied air force bombardment and constant ambushes and sabotage by the French resistance, so the units were unloaded farther east and had to reach the Normandy front by road, losing more valuable time. Only convoys with *Panzers* continued westward as did those with logistics train personnel. And so, on June 22, 1944,

I./SS-Pz.Rgt.1 was transferred aboard six transports and unloaded in the area east of Rouen.

A *Leibstandarte Panther* on a Paris street, June 1944.

A *Panther* of *I./SS-Pz.Rgt.1* on the march, 1944.

But these were only a few elements and not the entire unit. Other *Panthers* were unloaded north of Paris and some in the capital itself. As for the *II.Abteilung*, its elements were unloaded from tanks in the Saint-Cyr school sector, *Panzer* IVs from the *5.Panzer-Kompanie* were unloaded in Paris on June 21, and other units were unloaded just southwest of Caen. Once unloaded from the rail convoys, the *Panzers* had to reach the front by their own means and especially march at night to avoid Allied air attacks, which forced them to stay hidden

Waffen-SS tankers waiting to receive orders, 1944.

A *Waffen-SS Panther* on the Norman front, 1944.

An assault cannon completely covered with foliage.

in wooded areas during the day. The bulk of the *II.Abteilung* progressed along *Route Nationale 12* and reached Argentan from RN 24 around June 22. The following night, the battalion marched on the RN 158, crossed Falaise and turned west in the direction of the Cinglais Forest, between Bretteville-sur-Laize and Caen, where *the Leibstandarte* units were to regroup.

Employment in the Southern area of Caen

By July 1, 1944, *SS-Panzer-Regiment 1* was lining up 30 operational *Panzer IVs* and 25 *Panzer V Panthers*, while another 73 *Panzer IVs* and 38 *Panthers* were under repair. While some units of *1.SS-Pz.Div. 'LSSAH'* were engaged from June 29, *SS-Pz.Rgt.1* was placed in reserve in the rear of the Caen front in the first two weeks of July. As a result of new Allied attacks as part of Operation *'Jupiter'* launched by Marshal Montgomery, the *Panzer-Kompanien* of *II.Abteilung* set out between July 10 and 12 to be positioned for deployment in the perimeter of quota 112. Between July 15 and 17, the *I.Abteilung* of the *SS-Stubaf.* Kuhlmann took up positions east of RN 158, in the bocage sector near Secqueville. On July 16, the 2nd platoon of *5./SS-Pz.Rgt.1* under the orders of *SS-Ustuf.* Günter Pflughaupt had to support the *9.SS-Pz.Div. 'Hohenstaufen'* for an attack on Baron.

A *PzKpfw.IV* of the *Waffen-SS* in ambush position.

Crew of a *PzKpfw.IV* of the *Leibstandarte*, 1944.

Without prior reconnaissance and without adequate infantry support, the 4 *Panzer IVs* were destroyed in minutes in front of elevation 112. The next day, the regiment reported 59 *Panzer IVs* and 46 *Panthers* as operational. On July 18, the British launched Operation *'Goodwood'* by having it preceded by a massive air force bombardment, followed by equally massive preparatory fire from their artillery, hitting particularly the ground east and southeast of Caen. British tanks advanced behind the Caen-Paris rail line. *Panthers* of *I./SS-Pz.Rgt.1*, in position in the Bras-Bourguébus sector, confronted them at the foot of the Bourguébus ridge between Hubert-Folie and Soliers. The thirteen vehicles of the *2.Kompanie* under the orders of *SS-Ostuf*. Hans Malkomes managed to destroy 20 enemy tanks in a few minutes and invested the latter location. Around noon, the entire *I./SS-Pz.Rgt.1* was engaged between the positions of Bras and Bourguébus against the *11th Armoured Division*: some 40 enemy tanks were destroyed. The British Armored Division was pushed back across the railway line and left at least 126 destroyed vehicles destroyed by the various German units in the sector on the ground. *Leibstandarte Adolf Hitler's Leibstandarte*, for its part, lost a dozen *Panthers*. The line of ridges east of Bourguébus was clearly a target of the British, and defensive actions continued the next day: 2 well-camouflaged *Panthers* of the *4.Kompanie* successfully defended a high ground for several hours. On July 20, *Panzer IVs* of the 5. and 6./SS-Pz.Rgt.1 went into action in turn in this sector.

The commander of a *Panther* of I./SS-Pz.Rgt.1 observes the battlefield looking for enemy tanks during the fighting in Normandy, summer 1944 (*Michael Cremin Collection*).

SS-Ustuf. Werner Wolff (BA).

Two days later, *Panthers* of the *1.Panzer-Kompanie* of *SS-Hstuf.* Pötschke were engaged along RN 158 and continued on Ifs after penetrating an enemy front line. On July 25, the 2nd *Canadian Corps* launched Operation 'Spring'. The *Leibstandarte* repelled the Allied assaults on Tilly-la-Campagne, mainly engaging the *Panzers* of the *5.Kompanie*, which managed to inflict heavy losses on the attackers. Then, suddenly the front stabilized. By the evening of July 31, *SS-Panzer-Regiment 1* reported 61 *Panzer IVs* and 40 *Panthers* as operational, while 14 *Panzer IVs* and as many *Panthers* were under repair. On August 1, the Tilly-la-Campagne sector flared up again. The locality was heavily shelled, then two Canadian infantry battalions attempted to overrun it with tank support. But all the assaults were repulsed by the *Panzer IVs* of the *7./SS-Pz.Rgt.1* of *SS-Ostuf.* Werner Wolff, partly hidden in the rubble.

SS-Stubaf. Jochen Peiper.

A *PzKpfw.IV* in Normandy.

Numerous crews distinguished themselves in the course of the fighting, which lasted several hours. The fighting for this location continued for several more days. On August 2, *SS-Ostubaf.* Peiper left the front for health reasons. Officially, he complained of liver problems (he was suffering from liver disease), but it was actually nervous depression. The *SS-Stubaf.* Kuhlmann therefore resumed command of the regiment, replaced at the head of the *I.Abteilung* by the *Kompaniechef* of *1./SS-Pz.Rgt.1*, *SS-Hstuf.* Werner Pötschke. This change of command had no impact on the course of the subsequent fighting. In fact, the nature of the terrain, the Norman *bocage*, did not permit massive employment of German tanks, and the *Panzer-Kompanien* engaged their platoons individually in battle. Company commanders thus had little influence on the course of battles.

Mortain's counteroffensive

On August 5, *SS-Panzer-Regiment 1* reported 57 *Panzer IVs* and 46 *Panthers* operational. The *Leibstandarte* was taken over that same day to be regrouped north of Falaise. From this sector, the division was to reach a new front further west to confront the Americans and participate in the so-called '*Lüttich*' operation, also known as the Mortain counteroffensive. The objective was to cut off the American rear lines in the Avranches sector and isolate Patton's forces engaged south of the Cotentin Peninsula. The German offensive was launched on August 7, 1944: the *I.Abteilung* and the *5.Kompanie* of *SS-Pz.Rgt.1* were attached to the *2.Panzer-Division* southeast of Sourdeval. In the Saint-Barthélemy sector, operations did not unfold favorably for the *Panthers* of *SS-Hstuf.* Pötschke. The tanks were marching through a narrow path when an American plane swooped down on the leading *Panzer*, thus blocking the entire armored column. It took the *Panthers* two hours to extricate themselves from the created obstruction and resume their march toward their objective. The *1.Kompanie* under the orders of *SS-Ostuf.* Friedrich Christ went on the attack against Saint-Barthélemy, but a terrible American defensive fire blocked the *Panzers*. *SS-Hstuf.* Pötschke was personally engaged in the fighting and eventually the Americans abandoned the location under German pressure. The *I./SS-Pz.Rgt.1* then continued its advance southward, taking advantage of a thick mist, which, however, began to thin out soon after, favoring the intervention of Allied fighter bombers. The American divisions then went on the counterattack.

A *Leibstandarte Panther* engaged during the Mortain counteroffensive, 1944.

A *Panther* tank of the *Leibstandarte* in Normandy.

The next day, elements of *SS-Panzer-Grenadier-Regiment 2*, supported by some tanks, again attempted to penetrate the Saint-Barthélemy sector and reached Juvigny. But the German offensive was finally abandoned on August 10. In fact, following the penetration of the *3rd US Army* at Avranches, the threat of encirclement became real for the German units in the sector. The *1.SS-Panzer-Division 'LSSAH'* had to fall back eastward.

Falaise pocket

On August 12, the *Adolf Hitler Leibstandarte* was subordinated to *Panzergruppe 'Eberbach'* and found itself in the La Ferté-Macé sector. Its columns came under Allied artillery fire in the Domfront sector. As of August 13, the division lined up 14 *Panzer IVs* and 7 *Panthers* as operatives, with which it was to defend the La Ferté-Macé-Carrouges-Chahains line.

German *Panthers* engaged on the Normandy front, August 1944.

SS-Ostuf. Josef Armberger.

SS-Ostuf. Josef Armberger, commander of *8./SS-Pz.Rgt.1*, distinguished himself during the fighting with American forces in the Rânes and Mesnil-Angot sectors. Then the slow movement of the retreat continued under the protection of the regiment's last operational *Panzers*: on August 16, in the Faverolles-St.Georges-Rânes triangle, the remnants of *SS-Pz.Rgt.1* regrouped the next day in St.André-de-Briouze and St.Hilaire-de-Briouze, while other elements were already in Trun. Surrounded in the Falaise pocket, units of the *7.Armee* and *Panzergruppe 'Eberbach'* tried to escape from it as best they could. For the *Leibstandarte*, operations to exit the pocket began on the night of August 18-19. Between the 20th and 21st, most elements managed to fall back through the famous 'corridor of death' at Saint-Lambert-Coudehard. But *SS-Stubaf.* Herbert Kuhlmann was wounded in the course of the action and *SS-Ostuf.* Amberger, on the other hand was killed. Eventually, numerous *panzers* were abandoned along the road to Rouen, and few were the German vehicles that managed to be moved to safety on the other side of the Seine.

IX) New reorganization

After crossing the German border in late September, elements of *SS-Pz.Rgt.1*, under the orders of *SS-Hstuf.* Werner Pötschke, were among the first units to reach the Siegburg sector. The *I.Abteilung* was in Dellbrück, Holweide and Brück, near Cologne, while elements of the *II.Abteilung* were instead scattered among the localities of Birk, Geber, Bergisch Gladbach, Breidt-Deesen and Pohlhausen. In early October, the *Panzer-Regiment* set up its command post in Rahden, and the *Panzer-Kompanien* were deployed between Oppendorf, Oppenwehe and Wehdem.

SS-Ostubaf. Joachim Peiper, left, with other *SS-Pz.Rgt.1* officers during an official ceremony at Camp Rahden in November 1944. In the background is a *Panther* tank.

SS-Ostubaf. Peiper delivers decorations.

The *SS-Ostubaf.* Peiper left the Tegern hospital on October 7 and resumed command of the regiment a week later. Pötschke returned to the command of *I./SS-Pz.Rgt.1* and *SS-Hstuf.* Paul Guhl assumed command of the *II.Abteilung*. Instruction of the new recruits began immediately but lacked the material to reconstitute the unit. Peiper reorganized his regiment drastically, well aware that it would not receive all the expected tanks.

Leibstandarte Panzers 1940-1945

A *Flakpanzer IV 'Wirbelwind'* of the *10.Flak-Kompanie*.

A *Flakpanzer IV 'Ostwind'*, **November 1944**.

A mixed battalion (*gemischte*) was formed at Wietzendorf, near the Münster camp, with the *1.* and *2.Panzer-Kompanie* on *Panther* and the *6.* and *7.* on *Panzer IV*. A *10.Flak-Kompanie*, under the orders of *SS-Ostuf.* Karl-Heinz Vögler, was formed with two platoons equipped with two *Flakpanzer IV 'Wirbelwind'* and two *Flakpanzer IV 'Ostwind'* and a third platoon on *Sd.Kfz. 7/1* armed with a 20mm *Flakvierling* 38. The *9. (Pioneer)-Kompanie* remained under the orders of *SS-Ostuf.* Erich Rumpf. Finally, the *schwere SS-Panzer-Abteilung 501*, with its three companies on *Tiger II*, was again attached to the *LSSAH* regiment, as a replacement for the *II.Abteilung*, which could not be fully reorganized. Finally, worth mentioning is *SS-StuG.Abt.1*, also under the orders of *SS-Hstuf.* Karl Rettlinger, which was transformed at this same time into *SS-Panzerjäger-Abteilung 1*, as its assault guns were to be replaced with *Jagdpanzer IVs*, tank fighters built on *PzKpfw.IV* chassis and with a 75mm gun. On November 29, the division received its new orders: it was to participate in the '*Wacht am Rhein*' operation. As of December 1, *SS-Panzer-Regiment 1* reported 33 *Panzer IV* (out of the theoretical 109) and 34 *Panther* (out of the theoretical 79) operational, but more tank supplies were planned. Thirteen days later, *Leibstandarte* found itself at its starting positions in the Blankenheim Forest: Peiper learned that his unit would be the vanguard of the offensive. He was to take advantage of the surprise effect to bring up the enemy rear without worrying about protecting his flanks and reach the Meuse as quickly as possible, between Liège and Huy. The SS officer was assigned the command of a tactical grouping, the famous '*Kampfgruppe Peiper*,' comprising the *I./SS-Pz.Rgt.1* (*SS-Stubaf.* Pötschke), the *schwere SS-Panzer-Abteilung 501* (*SS-Ostubaf.* von Westernhagen), the *III.(gep.)/SS-Pz.Gren.Rgt.2* (*SS-Hstuf.* Diefenthal) and the *I.(gep.)/SS-Pz.Art.-Rgt.1* (*SS-Hstuf.* Kalischko). On Dec. 15, the day before the offensive began, the *I./SS-Pz.Rgt.1* had 37 *Panzer IVs* and 38 *Panthers* as operational, while *schwere SS-Panzer-Abteilung 501* received 11 additional *Tiger IIs* surrendered by *schwere Panzer-Abteilung 509*, what enabled it to line up a total of 45 armored vehicles.

X) The offensive in the Ardennes

On December 16, 1944, at 5:00 a.m., the last major German offensive on the Western Front was launched. On the *I.SS-Panzer-Korps* front, the units of the *12.Volks-Grenadier-Division* failed to pave the way for *Kampfgruppe Peiper* on time. The *SS-Ostubaf.* Peiper went on such a rampage that he could only give the order to attack at 4:30 p.m.: his tactical grouping finally reached Losheim at the end of the day. *SS-Ostuf.* Sternebeck, of the *6.Panzer-Kompanie*, had to bring himself to the head of the column, leading an armored vanguard (*Panzerspitze*) of 2 *Panther* and 5 *Panzer IVs*. Peiper, who did not want to waste any time, instead continued on to Lanzerath, where he arrived shortly before midnight.

Left, German armored units in an Ardennes village, waiting to move to attack, December 1944. On the right, a *Panther* of *SS-Pz.Rgt.1* on the march.

A Royal Tiger of *schw.SS-Pz.Abt.501* as it passes through the village of Tondorf on the eve of the offensive.

The paratroopers of *I./Fallschirmjäger-Regiment 9* were attached to *Kampfgruppe* as accompanying infantry. The tactical grouping later reached Buchholz, then Honsfeld, where 15 anti-tank pieces, 80 trucks and 50 Allied reconnaissance vehicles were captured. On the German side 2 *Panther* and 2 *Flakpanzer* were lost. The *Kampfgruppe* deviated from its planned route and passed through Büllingen to refuel its vehicles at an American depot. Peiper then returned to his assigned route and passed Möderscheid, Ondenval and Thirimont.

Elements *of Kampfgruppe Peiper* penetrate inside Honsfeld.

A *Flakpanzer IV 'Wirbelwind'* of *SS-Pz.Rgt.1* at Honsfeld.

Panther of *SS-Pz.Rgt.1* at the entrance to Stoumont.

The armored column then reached the Baugnez crossroads and captured 140 American soldiers from *Battery B* of the *285th Field Artillery Observation Battalion* after a short fight. The German tanks resumed their march toward Ligneuville, leaving some vehicles to guard the prisoners. Shortly afterwards gunfire was heard: 84 POWs were killed. The *SS-Stubaf.* Pötschke had certainly given the order to open fire; Joachim Peiper would be charged with war crimes for these executions after the war. *Kampfgruppe 'Peiper'* at that moment found itself dangerously fragmented and so was ordered to regroup immediately inside Ligneuville. The unit had meanwhile lost 3 *Panther* and 3 *Panzer IVs*, while another 8 *Panther* and 4 *Panzer IVs* were stranded due to mechanical failures. The *Tiger II* heavy battalion also complained of losses.

On Dec. 18, 1944, the attack on Stavelot was launched by *Panther* troops of *SS-Ostuf*'s *1./SS-Pz.Rgt.1*. Karl Kremser, with the town becoming the scene of violent fighting with American soldiers. The bridges over the Amblève River had been destroyed, so Peiper had to continue on to La Gleize, where *Kampfgruppe Knittel* was to establish liaison with him. But American units penetrated back into Stavelot, cutting Peiper's and Knittel's units off from their rear lines, thus isolating them completely!

A Royal Tiger of *Kampfgruppe Peiper* overtakes a column of American prisoners captured in the Ardennes.

A *Panther* of *Kampfgruppe Peiper* inside Stoumont.

A *Panther* commander orders the attack, December 1944.

On December 19, *Panther* units attacked Stoumont, but were blocked by a massive fire unleashed by enemy anti-tank pieces. Under fire, the *SS-Stubaf.* Pötschke went so far as to reprimand his subordinate, *SS-Ostuf.* Christ and his men, to let him resume the assault. Pötschke climbed back into his *Panther* to take the lead, but the attack was blocked again. In a fit of rage, he got out of his tank again, retrieved a *Panzerfaust* and threatened to pull on the retreating tanks! His gesture served its purpose: the *Panthers* managed to penetrate the city by firing: 150 prisoners, 4 anti-aircraft guns, 5 heavy anti-tank pieces and 4 *Shermans* were captured, after two hours of fighting. Impressed by Pötschke's behavior, Peiper would later recommend him for the granting of the Oak Fronds for his Knight's Cross. However, the conquest of Stoumont could not be exploited, as the *Kampfgruppe* was left without fuel and ammunition. Surrounded north of the Ardennes salient, its *panzers* were deployed around La Gleize in a defensive position. An attempt to resupply by air was unsuccessful, as was an attempt by *Kampfgruppe Hansen* over the river. At the end of the day on the 22nd, the *I.SS-Panzer-Korps* requested the withdrawal of *Kampfgruppe Peiper*, but the *6.Panzer-Armee* did not authorize it. The next day, Peiper decided to abandon all his equipment and walk to the German lines. His *Kampfgruppe* thus left 45 tanks (25 *Panther*, 10 *Panzer IV* and 10 *Tiger*), about sixty *SPWs* and other vehicles behind him.

Panther engaged in combat on the Ardennes Front, December 1944.

Joachim Peiper with the Knight's Cross with Oak Fronds and Swords.

With a thousand survivors, or one-third of its initial strength, the *SS-Ostubaf.* Peiper passed through the woods on December 24 and managed to reach the positions of the *I.SS-Panzer-Korps* east of Wanne. Despite not completing his mission, Peiper was recommended for the Swords for his Knight's Cross with Oak Fronds. Ultimately, only the 6. and 7.*Panzer-Kompanie*, as well as *the 1.* and *3./schwere SS-Panzer-Abteilung 501* had retained their assets since they had not crossed the Amblève River.

Officially disbanded on Dec. 26, 1944, *Kampfgruppe Peiper* claimed the destruction of 27 American tanks, 15 armored cars, 35 half-tracks, 14 aircraft, 50 heavy antitank pieces, 12 antiaircraft guns and 180 wheeled vehicles. Completely exhausted and very physically tested to be able to continue fighting, *SS-Ostubaf.* Jochen Peiper was again and temporarily assigned to the divisional staff. Beginning on December 27, Units of the *1.SS-Panzer-Division 'Leibstandarte Adolf Hitler'* were engaged in the Bastogne sector. In the field, *SS-Stubaf.* Pötschke resumed effective command of *SS-Pz.Rgt.1*, which had at that time 26 *Panzer IVs*, 16 *Panthers* and 33 Tigers of *s.SS-Pz.Abt.501* operational.

SS-Stubaf. **Werner Pötschke.**

German *panthers* engaged in the area south of Bastogne.

Grenadiers and *Panzers* in the Bastogne area, January 1945.

A destroyed *Jagdpanzer IV* in the Bastogne sector, 1945.

An attack was launched by *SS-Oberführer* Wilhelm Mohnke's division on December 30 with the aim of cutting through the Bastogne corridor. *Kampfgruppe Pötschke* captured the Lutrebois position, but the Americans soon after succeeded in blocking its movements with massive fire from their artillery and numerous attacks by their fighter bombers. The resumption of the German units' progression was similarly blocked the next day. Then the Americans in turn went on the attack and pushed back the German divisions. The losses suffered by *SS-Pz.Rgt.1* in the Bastogne sector were 7 *Panzer IV*, 4 *Panther* and 2 *Tiger II*. On January 10, 1945, the *Kampfgruppen* of the *Leibstandarte* were threatened with encirclement and were forced to fall back east of Saint-Vith. On January 15, the *Leibstandarte* was withdrawn from the combat zone and moved to the Cologne-Siegburg-Euskirchen-Bonn sector.

XI) On the Hungarian front

After the failure of the counteroffensive in the Ardennes, Hitler decided to transfer Sepp Dietrich's *6.Panzer-Armee* to the Hungarian front to protect the Nagykanisza oil fields, the last natural resources being indispensable for the continuation of the war. The reorganization of the *Leibstandarte* therefore had to be accelerated and took place between January 20 and 30, 1945. *The I./SS-Pz.Rgt.1* received the tankless crews of the *II.Abteilung* as reinforcements. At the same time, *SS-Ostuf.* Wolff assumed command of the *1.Kompanie* and the *SS-Hstuf.* Malkomes took over that of the *2.Kompanie*. As operational tanks there were 21 *Panzer IV* and 25 *Panther*, while another 9 *Panzer IV* and 10 *Panther* were under repair.

German armored units on the Hungarian plain during the first offensive actions in February 1945. In the foreground on the right is an *SdKfz.251* half-track armed with an anti-tank piece.

SS-Ostubaf. Peiper on the Hungarian front.

The order to move east came soon after. But by Feb. 1, only six convoys arrived in Hungary with elements of *SS-Pz.Rgt.1* and divisional staff. As of Feb. 12, 1945, the armored regiment reported 21 *Panzer IVs* and 34 *Panthers* as operational, to which 3 *Panzer IVs* and 2 *Panthers* under repair had to be added. A new supply of 10 *Panzer IVs* and 5 *Panthers* was also expected. *Schwere SS-Panzer-Abteilung 501*, also attached to *SS-Panzer-Regiment 1*, had 15 operational *Tiger IIs* and 11 under repair. On February 15, a *Panzergruppe* under the orders of *SS-Ostubaf.* Peiper was formed with the *I.(gemischte) Abteilung*, the *III.(gep.)/SS-Panzer-Grenadier-Regiment 2*, elements of the *I./SS-Panzer-*

Leibstandarte Panzers 1940-1945

Artillerie-Regiment 1 and the *s.SS-Pz.Abt.501*. The first German offensive in Hungary was launched on February 17 (Operation *Südwind*), but the motorized columns were immediately blocked by mud and snow.

Tiger II and half-tracks of *Panzergruppe Peiper* launched to attack on the Gran front, 1945.

Panther of the *Leibstandarte* on the Hungarian front, February 1945.

Despite everything, the units of *Kampfgruppe Peiper* and the *46.Infanterie-Division* eventually succeeded in capturing the western bank of the Gran Canal on both sides of the Giwa position. The next day, *Kampfgruppe Peiper* itself crossed the waterway and continued south to cut off the Köbölkut-Parkany road to the retreating Soviet forces. On the occasion, severe losses were inflicted on the enemy. The *Panzers* then stood in a defensive position for the night for a few hours of rest. On February 19, the *Panzergruppe* resumed its march and reached the Parkany road, suffering numerous attacks by Soviet fighter bombers. The next day, the *Panzergruppe* attacked along the Gran River and captured the Köhidgyarmat position on February 21. The *Panther* and *Tiger*, being of the most fuel-consuming tanks, eventually had to stop, awaiting supplies. On Feb. 25, *Leibstandarte* units began to leave the Gran sector to regroup north of Komàrom. At that time the *Panzergruppe* had 12 *Panzer IVs*, 11 *Panthers* and 4 *Tiger IIs* as operational.

Waffen-SS grenadiers and *panzers* during the fighting for the bridgehead on the Gran River.

A *Panther*, partially visible in the foreground, and a *Tiger II* of s.SS-Pz.Abt.501 engaged on the Hungarian front, 1945.

Operation "Spring awakening"

The *Leibstandarte* later reached the Veszprem-Zirc sector starting March 1 to participate in the Lake Balaton offensive, the main objective of which was to retake Hungarian oil wells captured from the Soviets. As of March 5, the *SS-Panzer-Regiment* was lining up 14 *Panzer IVs*, 26 *Panthers* and 15 *Jagdpanzer IVs*. All *Panzer IVs* came under the command of *SS-Ostuf.* Sternebeck. The offensive was launched on March 6. *Panzergruppe 'Pötschke'* got stuck 2 km west of elevation 149 and lost many vehicles to mines. The next day, Kaloz was captured from the south and continued north to support SS-Pz.Gren.Rgt.1 at Soponya. On March 9, the temperature dropped, causing mud to freeze on the roads, but the *Panzergruppe* was stranded after reaching the heights located around Janos Major. The following day, at least two *Panzer IVs* were destroyed in front of Simontornya. On March 11, the *Leibstandarte* still remained pinned down in front of this location despite an attempted coup by *SS-Ustuf.* Hermann Gerdes, launched with three *Panthers*. The latter spent the whole night in its midst fighting Soviet infantry after the destruction of the other two *Panthers*.

Panther Ausf. G of *I./SS-Pz.Rgt.1* marching on the Hungarian front, March 1945.

An *SdKfz.251* and a *PzKpfw.IV* of the *Leibstandarte*.

The following morning, the tanks of *SS-Ostuf.* Werner Sternebeck launched themselves against Simontornya firing all their weapons relentlessly: the locality was captured, but five *Panzer IVs* were destroyed. On March 16, having completely contained the German attacks, the Soviets launched a major counteroffensive between Bicske and Lake Velencze. The next day the German lines were penetrated and this marked the final end of the *6.Panzer-Armee* offensive in Hungary. In an attempt to close the breaches opened by the Soviets, *Heeresgruppe 'Süd'* ordered the intervention of the *I.* and *II.SS-Panzer-Korps* in this sector. To this end, the bulk of *SS-Panzer-Regiment 1* reached the area around Dég without too much trouble on March 18. At that time, Joachim Peiper's *Panzergruppe* still had 16 operational tanks and 38 others under repair, as well as 8 Tigers. The roads were clogged with the many retreating columns, along with fleeing civilians, under relentless Soviet artillery fire.

Waffen-SS grenadiers following a Royal Tiger during fighting in Hungary.

A *Panther* drives through a Hungarian village crossing numerous wrecks of destroyed Soviet vehicles and tanks, March 1945.

The commander of the *1.Panzer-Kompanie*, *SS-Ostuf.* Wolff, was hit by mortar shrapnel 2 kilometers from Inota while in the turret of his *Panther 101*. He died of his severe wounds on March 20. On this same day, *Kampfgruppe 'Sternebeck'* remained isolated further east with 6 *Panzer IVs* and 2 *Tigers* of *1./schwere SS-Panzer-Abteilung 501*, with no radio link to Peiper. By now all efforts of the *Leibstandarte* were in vain: Inota was captured by the Soviets. The *SS-Uscha*. Roman Clotten distinguished himself in his *Panzer IV* by destroying 7 tanks out of the 19 claimed by the 7./SS-Pz.Rgt.1. The SS division destroyed a total of 66 enemy tanks, but complained of as many losses on its part.

SS-Ostubaf. Heinz von Westernhagen.

SS-Hstuf. Hans Malkomes.

It was at this time that the *SS-Stubaf.* Kling assumed command of *schwere SS-Panzer-Abteilung 501*, replacing *SS-Stubaf.* Heinz von Westernhagen, who was killed shortly thereafter by Soviet artillery fire on his way to the armored corps command post. After the Soviets conquered Varpalota on March 21, the 16 tanks of *SS-Panzer-Regiment 1* established a defensive barrage on the Varpalota-Veszprem road with the remnants *of SS-Panzer-Grenadier-Regiment 1*. But they suffered a new hard blow when *SS-Hstuf.* Malkomes, commander of the *2.Kompanie*, was killed while in the turret at his *Panther*.

The next day, the 6th Guard Armored Army's attack clashed head-on with *Panzergruppe 'Pötschke,'* which had been ordered to keep the Veszprem road open at all costs. The next day was terrible for *SS-Pz.Rgt.1*, which lost four of its officers, including Pötschke, who was seriously wounded in the leg. He died the next day, refusing to have it amputated. All *Panthers* then came under the command of *the SS-Hstuf.* Otto and the *Panzer IVs* under that of the *SS-Hstuf.* Klingelhöfer. On March 27, the *Panzergruppe* launched one of its last counterattacks in the Noszlop sector.

On March 30, *Leibstandarte* units found themselves defending *Reich* territory. After falling back on Wiener Neustadt, they established a new and improvised defensive line there on the day of April 1.

Last fights in Austria

The *Panzergruppe* recovered 10 newly produced *Panzer* IVs at a station and launched a counterattack, blocking a Soviet armored formation at Katzeldorf and near Neudörfl. *SS-Ostuf.* Werner Sternebeck assumed command of the remnants of *the Leibstandarte* armored regiment. With the Soviets concentrated on conquering Vienna, the last elements of *SS-Pz.Rgt.1* repelled enemy attacks in the Pottenstein sector and Berndorf for several days. On April 8, *SS-Ostubaf.* Peiper reorganized his unit into three *Kampfgruppen*. The one personally commanded by him was engaged in the Hainfeld-Treisen sector with some

Leibstandarte Panzers 1940-1945

SS-Ostuf. **Werner Sternebeck.**

The *SS-Ostubaf.* **Peiper in Austria, 1945.**

Panther and *Tiger IIs*. *Kampfgruppe 'Kling,'* comprising some *Tiger IIs* of *s.SS-Pz.Abt.501*, crews of the *II.Abteilung* and other smaller units, was engaged in the Wilhelmsburg sector. *Kamfgruppe 'Sternebeck,'* comprising the last *Panzer IVs* of the 6th and 7th *Panzer-Kompanie*, was engaged in the Triesting valley, at Fahrafeld, Weissenbach, Neuhaus and Altenmarkt. On April 10, the Soviets launched a new offensive in the direction of St-Pölten. On the morning of the 13th, the *II.(gemischte)./SS-Pz.Rgt.1* of the *SS-Stubaf.* Guhl, without a single operational tank, arrived from Rahden to be engaged as an infantry unit. The next day, *Einsatzgruppe 'Peiper'* fell back to the Laaben-Stössing line. On the 18th, one of its last counterattacks from the Hainfeld sector resulted in the destruction of 15 enemy tanks. On the 19th, the Soviets attempted to take the *I.SS-Panzer-Korps* on its flank and forced the Germans to abandon Wilhelmsburg, despite the fact that *Einsatzgruppe 'Peiper'* had succeeded in locally blocking the attackers at Rotheau. On April 21, *Gruppe 'Kling'* fell back to Rotheau and Peiper's *Gruppe* fell back to Wiesental. The next day, the remnants of the *Leibstandarte* continued to retreat southward.

The end of the war was near: on May 2, on orders from the *I.SS-Panzer-Korps*, the front was held only by small *Kampfgruppen*. It was necessary to reach the demarcation line on the Enns River and surrender to the American units.

On May 8, the remnants of the *Leibstandarte* regrouped in the Scheibbs-Puchenstuben sector and from there reached Steyr, on the Enns, via Waidhofen and St-Peter. The *SS-Uscha.* Mayer recorded his last victory on a tank of the *1.SS-Panzer-Division* on that same day: it was his 22nd enemy tank destroyed during the war, most of them on his *Panther* of *1./SS-Pz.Rgt.1*. For his part, Peiper attempted to escape capture with his friend, *SS-Stubaf.* Paul Guhl, but fell into Allied hands near Schliersee on May 28, 1945.

Bibliography

- **Primary sources**

Public archives
Bundesarchiv Berlin Lichterfelde, Germany
Bundesarchiv-Militärarchiv Freiburg, Germany
U.S. National Archives Washington, U.S.

Magazines and publications of the time
Signal magazine, various editions and various issues
Das Schwarze Korps magazine, various issues

- **Secondary sources: published books**

On the Waffen SS in general
G. Bernage, "*Charkow. Le corps blindé contreattaque,*" Editions Heimdal, 1998
F. Duprat, "*Les campagnes de la Waffen SS,*" Les Sept Couleurs
Willy Fey, "*Armor battles of the Waffen-SS,*" Stackpole Books
P. Hausser, "*Waffen SS im Einsatz,*" Plesse Verlag, Göttingen 1953
R. Kaltenegger, "*The Mountain troops of the Waffen SS,*" ed. Schiffer
E. G. Kraetschmer, "*Die Ritterkreuztraeger der Waffen-SS,*" Preussisch Oldendorf 1982.
H. Landemer, "*The Waffen SS,*" Balland, 1972
R. Lumsden, "*The True Story of the SS,*" Newton & Compton Publishers.
K. Margry, "*The Four Battles for Kharkov,*" Num. 112 Series After the Battle.
Georg Maier, "*Drama zwischen Budapest und Wien,*" J. J. Fedorowicz Publishing, Inc.
G.H. Stein, "*The Waffen-SS: Hitler's Elite Guard at War 1939-1945,*" Cornell University Press
G. Tessin, "*Verbande und truppen der deutschen Wehrmacht und Waffen-SS,*" Biblio Verlag
C. Trang, "*Dictionnaire de la Waffen SS,*" Volume 1-4, Editions Heimdal
G. Williamson, "*Illustrated History of the SS,*" Newton & Compton publishers

On the *Leibstandarte Adolf Hitler*
Massimiliano Afiero, "*Leibstandarte SS Adolf Hitler 1933-1943,*" Ass. Cult. Ritterkreuz
Massimiliano Afiero, "*Leibstandarte SS Adolf Hitler 1943-1945,*" Ass. Cult. Ritterkreuz
P. Agte, "*Jochen Peiper, Kommandeur Panzerregiment Leibstandarte,*" Kurt Vowinckel Verlag
R. Butler, "*SS-Leibstandarte: the history of the first SS division 1933-45,*" Amber Books, 2001
T. Fischer, "*Das Panzer-Artillerie-Regiment 1 LAH an allen Fronten 1940-1945,*" Podzun-Pallas
T. Fischer, "*Von Berlin bis Caen. Entwicklung und Einsätze der Divisions-und Korps-Artillerie der LAH 1939-1945,*" Helios Verlag, 2004
R. Lehmann, "*Die Leibstandarte: vol.1-3,*" Munin Verlag, Osnabrück, 1977-1982
R. Lehmann, R. Tiemann, "*Die Leibstandarte: vol.IV/1-2,*" Munin Verlag, Osnabrück, 1986
R. Lehmann, "*Die Leibstandarte im Bild,*" Munin Verlag, Osnabrück, 1983
J. Lucas, M. Cooper, "*Hitler's Elite: Leibstandarte SS,*" Macdonald & Jane's, London 1975
K. Meyer, "*Grenadiers,*" J.J. Fedorowicz Publishing, 1994
G. Nipe, R. Spezzano, "*Platz der Leibstandarte,*" RZM Publishing, 2002
R. Tiemann, "*Chronicle of the 7.Panzer-Kompanie 1.SS-Panzer-Division 'LSSAH',*" Schiffer Publishing, 1998

C. Trang, "*Leibstandarte 1933-1942,*" Editions Heimdal
C. Trang, "*Leibstandarte 1943-45,*" Editions Heimdal
H. Walther, "*Die 1.SS-Panzerdivision,*" Podzun-Pallas Verlag, 1987
J. Westmeier, "*Joachim Peiper. A biography of Himmler's SS commander,*" Schiffer Publishing

Periodical publications
Der Freiwillige magazine: some issues
War Fronts magazine, bimonthly dedicated to Axis formations: some issues
Batailles & Blindés, Hors série number 31, "*Leibstandarte, Das Reich, Totenkopf, les régiments blindés de la SS-Panzerwaffe,*" September-October 2016, Caraktère SARL

- **Internet sites devoted to the German armed forces during World War II**

http://www.feldgrau.com
http://www.axishistory.com
http://www.lexikon-der-wehrmacht.de
http://www.okh.it
http://www.maxafiero.it
http://www.corazzati.it

- **Photographic references**

Ritterkreuz Cultural Association
Bundesarchiv, Germany (BA)
Washington, D.C. National Archives and Records Administration (NARA)
Berlin Document Center (BDC)
Ljubljana Institute of Modern History (MZNS)
Footage Deutsche Wochenschau (DW)
HTM Budapest
Imperial War Museum (IWM)
Munin Verlag

Private Collections
Maximilian Afiero
Michael Cremin
Maximilian Falconi
Horst Schumann
Pierre Tiquet
Charles Trang
Herbert Walther

CONTENTS

Leibstandarte Panzers 1940-1945 5
I) The assault guns of the LSSAH 7
    Eastern Front 9
II) The armored regiment 14
    Formation of the Panzer-Abteilung.. 16
    The Schwere Kompanie 19
    Departmental training and formation 20
III) On the Kharkov Front 23
    The reconquest of Kharkov 30
    The conquest of Bjelgorod 36
IV) Reorganization of departments 38
V) Operation Zitadelle 40
VI) Reorganization in Italy 47
VII) Return to the Eastern Front 50
    New fights 56
    The fights for Berditchev 62
    Fighting East of Vinnitsa 67
    On the Galician front 69
VIII) On the Western front 71
    Transfer to Normandy 73
    Employment in the Southern area of Caen 75
    Mortain's counteroffensive 78
    Falaise pocket... 79
IX) New reorganization 81
X) The offensive in the Ardennes 83
XI) On the Hungarian front... 88
    Operation "Spring awakening" 90
    Last fights in Austria 93
Bibliography.. 95

Leibstandarte Panzers 1940-1945

Leibstandarte Panzers 1940-1945

TITOLI PUBBLICATI - ALREADY PUBLISHING

Leibstandarte Panzers 1940-1945

www.ingramcontent.com/pod-product-compliance
Ingram Content Group UK Ltd.
Pitfield, Milton Keynes, MK11 3LW, UK
UKHW060214240426
12048UKWH00031BB/1714

9 791255 892519